GLIMPSES OF GOD

Lesley Carroll and Geraldine Smyth

Glimpses of
GOD

Reflections for Days and Seasons

VERITAS

Published 2010 by
Veritas Publications
7–8 Lower Abbey Street .
Dublin 1, Ireland
Email publications@veritas.ie
Website www.veritas.ie

ISBN 978 1 84730 094 2
Copyright © Lesley Carroll and Geraldine Smyth, 2010

10 9 8 7 6 5 4 3 2 1

A catalogue record for this book is available from the
British Library.

Cover Design by Norma Prause-Brewer
Printed in the Republic of Ireland by ColourBooks Ltd.,
Dublin

Veritas books are printed on paper made from the
wood pulp of managed forests. For every tree felled,
at least one tree is planted, thereby renewing natural
resources.

Contents

Advent & Christmas

Introduction

Fifty years ago, the Jewish philosopher, Martin Buber, spoke of the eclipse of God. But he rightly pointed out that 'a[n] eclipse of the sun is something that occurs between the sun and our eyes, not in the sun itself'.[1] In other words, it's not that God has disappeared, but that we have lost the art of paying attention. It is hard to keep praying into the silence and not be affected by God's seeming absence. The Dominican mystic, Meister Eckhart, seems to understand the plight of all ailing pray-ers. He wryly observed in one of his German sermons that when we pray and get no answer, it is not God who has gone out for a walk, but we ourselves.[2]

Many of us may be out of practice when it comes to praying, or maybe we have 'gone out for a walk' so to speak. We can nonetheless take heart from teachers like Martin Buber and Jacob Needleman that 'merely to look at things as they are, with bare attention, can be a religious act', a movement of grace. In so looking, we know that we are not alone, remembering with Dame Julian of Norwich that 'we are loved from the beginning'.

In this series of reflections, two women in faith – long-standing friends, one a Presbyterian minister, the other a Dominican sister – express something of their musings on what it means to pay attention to the glimpses of grace in life. All the times of our lives disclose unexpected moments of grace. Often we do not know the grace until the moment has passed, some time after the event, yet the ordering of our lives by God's grace is at the heart of our faith.

Noticing what is within and without is not easy. In our personal lives, there are times when we are stopped in our tracks — sometimes in joy, at times in sadness. In the life of a nation, there are times when its citizens need to pause and reflect. Some of the reflections were written at precisely those times and are drawn from the authors' experience of living through the conflict in and about Northern Ireland and the moves that have been made towards healing, peace and reconciliation.

The liturgical rhythm of the Christian Church invites stillness and attentiveness, and these twin dispositions set the tone for these thoughts and reflections. The book begins with the Lenten and Easter seasons: times when we are called to surrender to the way of the Suffering Servant so that we might share in the hope of the Resurrection. It ends with thoughts on Advent and Christmas: seasons which invite an awakening from the winter slumber of life to follow the newborn Christ who will 'make all things new' (Rev 21:5). The meditations in the days between these two high seasons form the body of the book and evoke the art and gift of meditative presence.

Originally broadcast on BBC as 'Thoughts for the Day' and adapted for this book, it is the authors' hope that their words may prompt the reader to pause, to lift the eye and to open the heart for glimpses of God in unsuspected places. They offer them in the hope that the reader might find hints here of what George Herbert, the seventeenth-century poet, spoke of as 'the soul in paraphrase, heart in pilgrimage ... Heaven in ordinaire ... something understood'.[3]

1   Martin Buber, *Eclipse of God*, New York and Boston, Harper and Row, 1952, 23.
2   *Meister Eckhart: Sermons and Treatises*, Vol. 1, Sermon 27 (Maurice O'Connell Walshe, ed. and trans.), Dulverton, Watkins Publishing, 1979, 207–209, 208.
3   George Herbert, 'Prayer', in *The Metaphysical Poets* (Helen Gardner, ed.), Harmondsworth, Penguin Books, 1957, 124.

About the Authors

Lesley Carroll, from Co. Tyrone, is currently Minister at Fortwilliam & Macrory Presbyterian Church, Antrim Road, Belfast. She is well known for her leading role in reconciliation and peace-building, and most recently as a member of the Commission on the Past, chaired by Archbishop Robin Eames and Denis Bradley. She completed her studies at the Irish School of Ecumenics, Trinity College Dublin, gaining a Ph.D. in Theology in 2007.

Geraldine Smyth OP is a Dominican sister and theologian from Belfast. She is a Senior Lecturer and Coordinator of the Research Degrees Programme at the Irish School of Ecumenics, Trinity College Dublin and a former director of ISE. Geraldine has a Ph.D. in Theology from Trinity College Dublin. She is a board member of Healing Through Remembering, a Belfast-based organisation focused on dealing with past conflict in and about Northern Ireland and shaping a new and peaceful society.

The paths of both women first intersected in 1993 when they came together to preach in Clonard Monastery, Belfast. The text that night was from St Luke (1:39-56), telling of Mary's visitation to Elizabeth. This gospel event was once described dramatically by Bishop Jeremy Taylor, the seventeenth century Anglican Archbishop of Armagh, as 'a collision of joys', and perhaps this is also an apt metaphor for the friendship of Lesley and Geraldine and their continuing exchange of gifts in the Irish School of Ecumenics and beyond. The authors are appreciative of the wisdom and professional guidance of Rev. Dr Bert Tosh, Head of Religious Broadcasting in BBC Northern Ireland, who, with Chandrika Nayar and the BBC team, enabled the two women to share their reflections with a wider audience of listeners through the Thought for the Day programme.

Lent & Easter

Spring Rain

Geraldine Smyth

Some years, Lent seems to steal up on me unawares, and it can be hard to stifle a groan, with the association of confronting our sins and doing penance. But then I remember that Lent is a first cousin of Spring, the word 'Lent' deriving from the Old English word for Spring. Maybe it is truly understood as being not so much about self-denial and harsh penances, as about the creative thrust within us towards healing and hope. There is within all of life an impulse towards renewal. The ancient symbols of sackcloth and ashes remind us of our need for God's newness and symbolise the reality that we are about to leave behind all that is dead and old in our lives, and make the transition to a new way of living. Lenten renewal can come to birth in the digging of soil and planting of seeds, in singing or listening to music, or in giving time to a neighbour or donating alms to those in need. It is a time for opening our scriptures with fresh expectancy, a time for simplifying our needs, for living more basically so that others might simply live. Perhaps such an approach can give a new context to the ancient Lenten practices whose remnants linger around us. Lent is a time not so much about getting a stoical grip on our human nature, as about treating ourselves to those very things we miss and desire in the arid, concrete maze of modern life – delight in nature, poetry, silence and prayer: God's free gifts.

Doubtless, Lent offers stark reminders of our own shame and sin, and calls us to go into the desert places where we may catch a glimpse of God's back and know something of God's otherness. Small wonder that behind the discomfort this evokes lurks a fear at the prospect not simply of complacency dislocated, but of encounter with the awesome tremendousness of God. Lent may well be about seedtime and new life, but it is also a disturbance. Like a sudden Spring, it comes shaking nature out of its hibernation. It is in the nature of Spring to dislodge us from the lethargy induced by winter. T.S. Eliot glimpsed that truth when he wrote:

> *April is the cruellest month, breeding*
> *Lilacs out of the dead land, mixing*
> *Memory and desire, stirring*
> *Dull roots with Spring rain.*[1]

Lent, likewise, sets our barren memory astir with new desire, breaks open our sealed lives with alternative visions. This Lent, let the sap rise, let all the numbed-over parts of our bodies and minds feel the rinsing, wringing touch of the Creator God. With another poet, we too cry out:

> *Mine, O thou Lord of life, send my roots rain.*[2]

---

1   'The Wasteland', in *T.S. Eliot: The Complete Poems and Plays*, London and Boston, Faber and Faber, 1969, 61–75, 61.
2   Gerard Manley Hopkins, 'Thou art indeed just, Lord', in *Selected Poems of G.M. Hopkins* (James Reeves, ed.), London, Heinemann, 1967 (1953), 75.

Great Escape

Geraldine Smyth

The escape of the Israelites from slavery in Egypt is a story that evokes hope in the hearts of oppressed peoples everywhere. Stories about escape have always engaged and sustained people, whether escapes from prison or concentration camp or tyrannical regime. Films like *The Great Escape, The Fugitive* or *The Shawshank Redemption* are modern-day epics of freedom and the dramatic risks that people take to protect or regain that freedom.

But escape has its less heroic side. Thoughts of escape are what spring into my mind when I see someone I want to avoid, or anticipate a meeting fraught with conflict. These days, spring-cleaning – the thought of clearing out that drawer, so bunged up it won't close, or of bringing the pile of newspapers to the recycling bin – prompt escape plans of epic proportions. The thought that I might go for an early morning run or deal with letters is enough to propel me into the inertia of busyness or lull me into the inertia of laziness. The old word used for inertia was 'sloth', and the new American term for us slothful ones is 'couch potatoes'. In older Ulster idiom we would have been said to have been as 'lazy as *sioch* water'. My mother's unimpressed comment on my absorption in a book every time 'dishes' were mentioned still smarts: 'That one wouldn't turn her toe where her heel was.' Never was a more withering judgement on bone idleness delivered in such economy of phrase.

Lent invites us to let go of our escapades of avoidance and look freedom in the eye. Lent faces us with our fear of freedom. That is the burden of John the Baptist's call: 'The time has come and the kingdom of God is close at hand. Repent and believe the good news.' Give up turning a blind eye and quit turning a deaf ear, stop being as lazy as sin, he is saying, and start turning your toe where your heel is. Lent is a time of shaking up, shaking off, shaking out, and of turning our minds and hearts from the old comfort zones towards riskier freedoms of the untried and the new.

Few have realised better than Nelson Mandela that the road to freedom can be a long one. Describing his thoughts and feelings on the day he walked free from prison after twenty-eight years, Mandela speaks of newness: '… as I finally walked through those gates I felt – even at the age of seventy-one – that my life was beginning anew.'[1] In Ireland, we have had too many years of closed walls and communities often sealed off in solitary confinement from one another. Mandela's words encourage us now, too, to walk on in the freedom of people who belong to one another: 'We will walk the last mile together.'

1 The Long Walk to Freedom: The Autobiography of Nelson Mandela, London, Little, Brown and Co., 1994, 553.

Breaking Bread

Geraldine Smyth

Food – and our lifelong involvement with it – is at the core of how we relate to ourselves, others, animals and to nature itself. Around food revolve the most vital dramas of survival, economics, relationship with the earth, communion with others or with God. Lent, Ramadan, Passover: food – and our relationship to it – symbolises that most fundamental pattern in life; one of exchange, of giving and receiving.

We have seen peoples die of starvation because of closed markets, rigged prices, or confiscation of land. We have witnessed the ironies of famine and food mountains; starvation and slimming diets. There are daily reports of pollution in our seas and rivers, interference with the food chain – from DDT to PCP, BSE, CJD, E.COLI.

The film *Babette's Feast* is a story of how food turns enemies into friends, restores broken trust and replenishes delight in beauty, goodness and desire. Babette, once a master-chef in Paris, fleeing from war in her country, arrives, in the opening scene, on the bleak shores of Jutland. Collapsing in a state of exhaustion on their doorstep, she is taken in by two ageing sisters whose father had been the strict village pastor. Her past remains a secret and they do not pry. Years later she wins the French lottery, and in one prodigal gesture expends it all on the creation of a lavish meal for the dispirited villagers. One by one, thinly veiled resentments and jealousies that had festered over the years are acknowledged; the pain of opportunities squandered is expressed and redeemed. Stories told around the table somehow rekindle a delight in life and compassion for others in the lack and losses that have marked their lives. The meal becomes a sacrament of abundant life and reconciliation. As they partake in it, the difference between hosts and guests disappears and God's love among them is renewed.

During Lent, we remember Jesus' journey into the wilderness with only wild beasts for company, eating only of the fruits of the wilderness. Lent questions our choices about food; the way food includes or excludes; the appalling vista of hunger that afflicts so many millions of the human family. Lent, whether through fasting or feasting, is about life and about reconciliation. For Christians, with their memory of Jesus' farewell meal or 'Last Supper', and of his constant example of sharing meals with outcasts and strangers, it is an opportune time for reflecting on our own lacklustre hospitality, on who it is that we debar from food and friendship, and why we are not more troubled that the day has not come when we can gather together in companionship at the Lord's Supper.

Unforsaken

Lesley Carroll

They say a mother's life isn't easy. A life shot through with joy and sorrow, not knowing each day whether, at the end of it, it will be the joy or the sorrow that comes out on top. Once a year or so we celebrate our mothers, but mostly we are grateful for what they do in an unspoken, unconcerned kind of way.

Of course, some mothers have more than others to bear. As if it wasn't enough for Mary, the mother of Jesus, to watch her son pursue a lifestyle that would cause many to speak ill of him, question him or admire him for all the wrong reasons — as if all that wasn't enough, Mary was going to find herself standing at a place called Golgotha, watching her son being crucified.

As each nail was put in place and the physical pain registered on her son's so familiar face, a face she had learned to read when he was only a baby in her arms, I wonder did she remember her own pain, the physical pain of childbirth that had brought him into the world? I wonder did she remember and ask herself, has it come to this? Or did her own pain fade into nothing as she felt and shared the present pain of her son? Did it almost overwhelm her? Was she able to stand at all or did the pain she felt, this new, uninvited pain which anticipated no joy at its ending, did this pain drag her to the ground?

At least there were other mothers around her. Women who could imagine the torture of their friend Mary; women who were relieved that they did not have to watch their sons die. Did Salome think of the sons she had borne with Zebedee? Did another Mary think of her sons James and Joses? Did they reach out to touch Mary the mother of Jesus or were they too overwhelmed by the grief they shared and could do nothing about?

There at the foot of the cross were many burdened by unimaginable grief. There is still a place for all whose burden of grief is so great that they can hardly stand up; mothers, fathers, children, and single people too, those who watch and wait with the dying, those whose watching and waiting is done. God hasn't forgotten you, for the grieving have always been gathered at the foot of the Son's cross. All who are grieving are in full view of the Son of God.

At the Foot of the Cross

Lesley Carroll

Seven demons had been cast out of her. Jesus had seen to that. But what demons remained for other people, for people are not generally as kind as Jesus was, and they did not easily forget. Back in Magdala, she probably thought, they likely still talked about the miracle but forgot that she had been changed, forgot to open their arms to one they remembered as demoniac. Mary Magdalene's private agonies remained just that – private. For no one ever thought to write them down. Miracle there might have been but no one thought to record the detail for this demoniac's new life.

One short record, in the gospel of Luke, hints at what the days after her healing might have been like. When Jesus travelled from one town and village to another he was accompanied by the twelve disciples and also by some women, all of whom had experienced some kind of healing. They were an interesting lot. Some were well connected, like Joanna, whose husband, Chuza, managed King Herod's household. Mary Magdalene was among them, but mostly they go unnamed. They travelled with the well-known twelve and their teacher Jesus, supporting them out of their own pocket and seeing to their needs. In their quiet, unrecognised way, they lived discipleship.

Mary Magdalene, I imagine, never expected to be remembered. Most disciples, focused on the task of following, don't think much about whether or not their names will go down in history. I suspect that she didn't expect either to find herself at the foot of a cross, watching the horrific death of the one who had renewed her life. Maybe at the foot of the cross the memories returned of the days when the people of Magdala had teased and scorned her. Maybe at the foot of the cross those memories mocked her once more as people laughed at and taunted Jesus.

There was a place for Mary Magdalene at the foot of the cross, a privileged place, where disciples are found. There is a place at the foot of the cross alongside Mary Magdalene for all who have suffered mocking and scorn, for all whose healing has gone unnoticed, for all whose discipleship is almost forgotten, almost overlooked.

Communion of Saints

Lesley Carroll

When they lay me in my grave, I sometimes wonder, what will people remember? Will they remember anything? How long until I, like so many before me, become a name on a headstone, a faceless person, my history and all my sophisticated plans and marvellous visions buried with me. It doesn't depress me any more to think like that. It doesn't make me want to be great or long to do something that history can't ignore – like Marie Curie or Amy Johnston or Florence Nightingale.

It doesn't depress me because I know that I will be in good company. I will be in the company of the many women who have lived faithful, eventful and effective lives and have never been written about in history's grand tomes. I will be in the company of the nameless, faceless women who followed Jesus on his way of sorrow, the daughters of Jerusalem who wept and mourned before he even came to the place of the Skull.

I will be in the company of the many women who gathered around the cross, watching and waiting with the Son of God as he faced death, watching and waiting not through a hiccup in the history of the world but watching over the event which would turn history around forever. Watching as a new age came to birth. And what interesting company I think these women will make – from all walks of life, with all kinds of savoury and unsavoury experiences, all with stories to tell. I will be in the company of the women who had come from Galilee with Jesus, and who had the courage to go with the brave Joseph of Arimathea to see where the body was laid, and then go and prepare spices and perfumes with which to anoint the body.

Only a name on a gravestone? A faceless person? I will be in great company. And when I gaze across the company of strangers, this company of unacknowledged souls, there will be many women but also men there too. Men who chose servanthood like their Lord. Men who suffered and struggled and felt ignored. Men about whom no one has ever written. We will be a great company of people, people who began at the foot of a cross. A company of nameless, faceless people who are known to God.

Dead Man Walking

Geraldine Smyth

Listening to a radio interview with Sr Helen Prejean on her campaign for the abolition of capital punishment, called to mind the controversial film based on her story, *Dead Man Walking*, about her friendship with a prisoner on death row. It was, at a most profound level, a story of sin and suffering, and it grappled with the human and divine possibility of forgiveness and reconciliation.

The film centres on Matthew Poncelet, awaiting the death penalty for the rape and murder of two young sweethearts. At frequent intervals in the film, the crime is revisited in brutal flashback. Helen becomes his prison visitor, spiritual guide and advocate, urging him to take responsibility for his own past, even while she challenges the system and the prevailing culture of revenge. Encountering the parents of the murdered victims and the well of grief within them, she knows their anger and their sense of being trapped somewhere between devastation and despair. She comes to recognise her over-simplified view of pardon, and finds herself standing in a place of contradiction.

The tension between forgiveness and revenge is excruciating. No position is un-examined, the boundaries between sinners and sinned-against keep shifting, and ultimately, innocence and guilt must let go to grace. At the end, Helen is there for Matthew, sustaining him with the words of Isaiah: 'If you stand before the power of hell and death is at your side, know that I am with you through it all.' The final drama in the execution room reveals the interweaving of grace and disgrace in our world, and discloses that the grace of Christ's reconciliation touches us through the concern and compassion of one another.

In John's gospel, we read of another woman, Martha of Bethany, who intercedes with Jesus for her brother. Lazarus was not in prison as such, but dead – in the tomb for four days. Martha believes that Lazarus will rise again and she confesses Jesus as the Son of God. This Lenten day, we take the words she heard to ourselves and to what has gone dead in our faith: 'Lazarus come forth!', and then 'Unbind him!' (Jn 11:43-44) Whatever is captive in us too will be set free. In gospel story and film alike, we discover that we are called as sisters and brothers to unbind one another. As we walk in the light of the Resurrection, the notion of 'Dead Man Walking' becomes a radical, astonishing possibility.

New Life

Geraldine Smyth

Advertising used to work around the edges of life, and you were always well warned by parents and teachers not to be taken in. Nowadays, its hidden persuasion comes at you everywhere, hitting you between the eyes as you try to watch reality TV in peace! Ads on the back of buses, neon signs changing messages every ten seconds, high rise word-bites striking from billboards urging whiter teeth and still whiter clothes, messages that condemn the wilful neglect of your drab hair – because you're worth it. Others offer comfort to your ecologically-disastrous lifestyle, telling you that your petrol fumes, far from piercing a hole in the ozone layer, are responsible for purifying, not putrefying the earth, cleansing the air, making rivers run clean, flowers spring green – all because your petrol company cares about the planet, and is daily planting trees beside the oil wells. The marketing world displays its newly discovered concern with the inner life – even consumerism needs its spirituality. So too with the increasingly common 'green' ads aimed at elevating our aspiration with images of the hidden essence – of cleanness, wholeness, faith in the power of multinational companies to renew the face of the earth.

Some advertisements filch words and phrases from the Bible to proclaim their message in sanctified tones: one has only to BELIEVE and thirst will be no more; BELIEVE and victory will be won as we prepare once more for the coming of the Titan team in the latest cup series. I remember a soft drink, long-advertised for its recuperating properties, which was given a makeover one year, popping out of hoardings everywhere around Eastertime. Playing subliminally on the message of resurrection, the familiar red and yellow bottle now emerged triumphant, bursting forth from an egg, the caption proclaiming, 'Energy from within'. Christ in a bottle bursting from the tomb. The image may well evoke irritation in the breast of your average Christian, but that for me changed to a chuckle at the way the Easter story never ceases to re-invent itself; at the way these ancient symbols of creation and new creation break out and insist on new beginnings – in a time when God is rumoured dead. Donegal poet, Moya Cannon, in her poem 'Easter Houses', recreates her childhood Easters and the urge to be out in the open in that Easter house 'that never had a roof'. The eternal newness of life breaks through in every insistent line:

After the battened-up heart of winter,
The long fast of spring,
Life had come out again to nest in the open;
Again the shell was chipped open from within.[1]

___

1   'Easter Houses', in The Parchment Boat, Oldcastle, Gallery Books, 1997, 31.

Beyond Loss

Geraldine Smyth

Week by week, in season and out, we are surrounded by sport and by the media spectacle of the hungry ambition for winning and the dire costs of losing. Almost always, one thing is certain sure: for every match played, one team will lose the contest, and after a few losses, one hapless manager will lose face, and likely thereafter, his job. And yet if we stop and think, loss is not always about defeat. Its opposite is not always victory. It is a word with many opposites: we speak of loss and discovery, loss and recovery, loss and gain, of lost and found. Jesus himself told his disciples that those who lose their life for his sake would find it. At Easter, we sing an ancient hymn of Jesus who suffered upon the cross to redeem our loss.

Loss, lose, lost are among the most hard-worked words in the language. We speak of lost time, a lost cause, a lost hope. In this ecological age, we conserve water and recycle paper, rather than see them go to loss. Whenever we go to sympathise with a bereaved family, we can find ourselves at a loss for words, and fumble for the trusted ritual, 'I'm sorry for your loss'. Loss is a state of lack, something missing, an absence. Loss evokes strong feelings – frustration, grief, anger, confusion – and can make a person desperate.

Do you ever lose your rag with your teenage offspring who seem so eager to get out in the world and lose their innocence, or your money, while telling you in their own cool idiom to 'get lost'? With rising inflation, we hear of companies making a loss, and if things go from bad to worse, the loss-adjustors will be in.

As a teenager, it was a matter of long suffering to me every time I announced my latest loss to the universe – 'Where is my school-bag? my book? my tennis racquet?'

only to hear the unsympathetic response, 'It's wherever you left it!' Not true. There be gremlins. Whatever about our childish carelesness about the whereabouts of our stuff, often now amid the confusion or loss, we are just looking in the wrong place or fighting the fact that life does not stay the same.

That was the way with Mary Magdalene. She went to the tomb, expecting to find Jesus' body there where it had been buried. She bends down, looks inside, but finds that the tomb is empty. Her loss is measured by her tears. But she was looking in the wrong place. She was looking to the wrong thing. She expected it would be just so, and it was quite other. 'Woman, why are you weeping?' ask the angels. 'They have taken away my Lord and I do not know where they have laid him' (Jn 20:13). She was at a loss with grief. But it was in that very loss that Jesus found her and called her by name, 'Mary!' (vs 16). She turned around, and in this turning around, her life changed forever. In telling her not to cling to him, Jesus asks her to let go of what is lost – the bodily reality she once knew, the routines between them which had already re-shaped her identity. That is gone and lost; this risen stranger points her life and purpose in a whole new direction. Beyond this loss, she will find herself anew, no longer as companion, but as Apostle entrusted with the Resurrection message.

What are we looking for? What if we believed that nothing really precious will be lost in the letting go? What if we trusted everything lost will be found again strangely transfigured in a new light – by the One who says, 'See, I am making all things new' (Rev 21:5)?

The Days of
Our Lives

Stand Still

Geraldine Smyth

'Stand still and you're history!' Thus announced a roadside billboard that recently caught my eye. I stood warned. It was an advertisement for the latest in information technology. 'Stand still and you're history!' A stern statement on the undesirability of being left behind, on forging ahead as the key to communication. Standing still is bad; history is for the losers.

How well we know the demand to keep moving, to pass ourselves out. Too familiar are we with pumping heart and tightening chest. So we accelerate the pace and raise the stakes for staying in control. Better the two-mile detour than two minutes immobile in a traffic queue; the illusion that to keep moving anywhere is better than standing still. So we work longer hours, maintaining the advance progressively backwards.

A wise teacher once said that there are two ways of looking at life: there is the look of the arrow and the look of the cup. Mostly, in the West, we live life by the look of the arrow – narrowing the aim, whizzing to the target; taut, driven, single-minded. With the look of the arrow, we are propelled by the anxiety to get it right.

The other way of looking at life is with the look of the cup. With this look, we open our eyes to contemplate what surrounds us, to heed the world's sorrow or hope. With the look of the cup, we become part of life's exchange, its giving and receiving. Our vision expands and lets go of views that narrow down and exclude. Looking at life with the look of the cup, we welcome the music of what happens.

Jesus bade his disciples to be gentle with themselves, gentle towards one another, inviting them to learn the rhythms of nature, to consider the lilies of the field that neither toil nor spin. Jesus' own life became the cup poured out for all, the cup of blessing shared with us.

'Come to me,' he says, 'all you that labour and are heavy-burdened, and I will refresh you. Take up my yoke and learn from me, for I am gentle and humble of heart. And you will find rest' (Mt 11:28-30).

So, before we rush into the day's cares, gathering into barns, keeping score, generally striving to earn a crust – we stand still. Before focusing our concentration with the look of the arrow, we welcome the day as it comes, and open our eyes with the look of the cup:

> Teach us to care and not to care
> Teach us to sit still
> Even among these rocks,
> Our peace in His will ...[1]

---

1   T.S. Eliot, 'Ash Wednesday', in T.S. Eliot: The Complete Poems and Plays, op. cit., 89–99, 98.

A Place in the Sun

Geraldine Smyth

One of my favourite TV programmes that carries me far into the land of escapism is *A Place in the Sun*. The format is simple – a person or couple with money to spend on a holiday-home away from home are helped by a guide who has identified properties to be visited. And so, I journey with them as they consider their options on properties located in some beautifully situated spot in the Auvergne or Cephalonia, imbibing and savouring something of the local context and culture, spying out the land for a restored eighteenth-century villa, a beach-front apartment, or a mountain retreat.

The house-hunters are generally desirous of finding a place of tranquillity, away from what they describe as 'the rat race' of their workaday world; or on the threshold of retirement, contemplating a home away from home – in a house with an arresting view, in a place where the rhythm of life runs slow and a gentler work-life balance can be recovered.

This need for seasonal balance – daily, weekly, annually – is written deep in the human psyche. The call to re-finding oneself, returning to the centre, or simply ensuring that the demands of work are kept in check and in proportion to other needs, values and visions, is enshrined in every religious tradition. It may be through daily meditation or chanting of psalms; wilderness experiences and times of fasting; festive meals, liturgical music and dance that bear witness to the divine in the midst of life. There are rich and varied traditions of going on pilgrimage or on retreat in a place of sanctuary to give time to praise and thanksgiving or to make intercession for our own and others' needs. In the multi-religious world around us, who hasn't heard of the deep symbols of Divali, or Eid or Pentecost, that still invite us to cross the threshold and enter the dangerous, yet protected space of encounter with the divine Other.

The much beloved 23rd psalm envisages for us such a quiet space and time: green pastures; still waters; an outspread feast; cup overflowing; and the soothing anointing of the head – a vision of body, soul and spirit restored that no earthly spa or place in the sun could hope to match.

The Jewish tradition of Sabbath is another such deep symbol of God abiding with us. The Sabbath calls us into God's space of rest and delight in the works of creation. It supports us as we listen deeply to the rhythm of God's love and holiness pulsing through the whole living universe. Rabbi Heschel described Sabbath as 'a sanctuary in time', as 'eternity in the midst of time'.[1] It helps us to see with God's wide perspective; Sabbath is a room with a transcending view; a house built on rock where we can put our own cares in proportion and open the doors of hospitality to others. Shall we perhaps then feel the gentle breeze of the divine Spirit that blows within us, around and beyond us, from the rising of the sun over the mountain to its setting at the sea's furthest end.

---

1 Abraham Joshua Heschel, The Sabbath: Its Meaning for Modern Man, with wood engravings by Ilva Schor, Boston, Shambhala Press, 2003 (1951), xvii, 5, 68, 92.

Meeting Places

Geraldine Smyth

Have you noticed nowadays how everyone is talking about space – needing space, asking others to give them space, or stopping others from invading it? We have come to see 'space' as the condition of well-being. Before, we had no time, but now, we have no space. In the open-space technology of the market, people under pressure speak of 'claiming their space' as if it were a commodity. Books on Feng Shui are all the go; gurus tell us that clearing out our closets will open up our souls. Clarifying our life-spaces is cultivated to an art form, marketed as the antidote to all our getting and spending.

Yet, beyond the consumer's guide to sacred space, are we perhaps trying to recover the dwindling space in our culture for prayer and the intimacies of silence or simple conversation? Are we saying that in home or city we need a place to be – somewhere where noise can cease, where we can listen for the music of the Spirit? Earlier generations left a legacy of soaring cathedrals, spacious parks and hospitable public squares. These embodied in glass or stone the vision and values of life as civic, communal and spiritual. Some say we will bequeath to future generations the glass-domed shopping mall and glass towers of financial enterprise. These are the post-modern places of commerce and worship. They mock the human longing for intimacy and for mystery. Many urban buildings are made of glass – with the illusion that what goes on inside is transparent. Foyers simulate public squares or crossroads; a synthetic fountain replaces the well. Signposts point the way to departments or restaurants. But nobody gathers at the fountain or speaks with the passing stranger. No Ancient Mariner tugs at your sleeve with a yarn to tell.

Such characters have been seen off, leaving us adrift from real community, deprived of the spiritual nourishment of deep symbols – with the 'tragedy of a starved imagination'.[1]

The prophet Isaiah, writing for a people in exile, proclaimed that there was a home for them in God's imagination:

> Ho, everyone who thirsts, come to the waters; ... Come, buy wine and milk without money and without price! Why do you spend your money for that which is not bread ... Eat what is good and delight yourselves in rich food. Incline your ear, and come to me. (Is 55:1-3)

A thought to ponder as you head off to the bank or shopping centre, or clear the boot to make space for the school bags.

---

1   Paul Claudel, 1926, cited in Gabriel Daly, 'Catholicism and Modernity', *Journal of the American Academy of Religion*, 1985, LIII (4), 773–796, 773.

Foolish Shadows

Lesley Carroll

There is nothing like falling into bed exhausted, going immediately to sleep and waking in the morning refreshed and ready for a new day. From time to time, however, I am troubled by sleepless nights, and there is little worse than lying awake knowing that you really need to be asleep. During one recent long, sleepless night, I pulled a book of fables from the shelf and was struck by their simplicity but also by their hard-hitting truth.

Aesop, of course, is probably the greatest name associated with fables. He told this story about the wolf and his shadow. One evening, while the sun was sinking in the sky, a wolf wandered across a plain. As he wandered he noticed his shadow and became impressed by its size. He was so impressed that he said to himself, I didn't know I was so big. Imagine me being afraid of a lion. I, and not he, should be known as the King of Beasts. The wolf was so puffed up with his own importance that he carelessly became heedless of danger. As he strutted around admiring himself and preening himself, a lion suddenly sprang upon him and began to tear him limb from limb. The wolf soon changed his tune, crying, if only I hadn't lost sight of the facts, I wouldn't have been ruined by my fancies.

Foolish imagination and foolish pride can tempt our eyes away from the facts about ourselves, facts which are only too plain for others to see. There are times when the facts are without charm. But the truth of the matter is that we are always much safer with the facts than we are with puffed-up pride and foolish fancy.

While it is important for us to be aware that we have an easily inflated ego, it is also worth asking ourselves why we feel that we would rather be something other than what we are? That is a more important question. Why was the wolf discontented with himself? Discontented with ourselves we can be slow to see the advantages and strengths of our own personality and experience.

Today it may well do us good to listen to what others say about us but to especially listen to the positives and not to the negatives. It helps us to accept ourselves and even to begin to rejoice in ourselves, and it holds back the temptation to think of ourselves in fanciful ways. We are who we are. God made us that way, and as the Book of Genesis reminds us, when God looked at all that had so carefully and lovingly been made, God saw that it was all very good.

Choices

Lesley Carroll

As we rise each morning, we can face a day crammed full with decisions. We will have to contend with our reactions to other people and with their reactions to us. For some, the day will be well punctuated with time and space to think; to remember and to dream for the future. Others will be lucky to have a few minutes' breathing space to remember that life really is a blessing. We know some of the things this day holds for us but, like every other day, there is room for surprises.

When evening comes we will be able to look back on this day and decide if what we have done or said was based on what is really important in life. Did the way we disciplined our children, spoke to our parents, noticed our neighbours, dealt with our colleagues, reflect what is important for us at the very core of our being? At the end of this day, will we ask ourselves whether or not we have nurtured our core commitment, making it stronger and more alive and more visible to others?

Let me share a Chinese fable with you. It is written with regard to the way kings in Mongolia shared out newly conquered land with the subjects of the kingdom:

A man was entitled to stake his claim to newly conquered land and this claim was made by riding on horseback across as much land as possible between the hours of sunrise and sunset. After a campaign when much land was conquered, one man galloped off as dawn broke. He rode due north until midday, when he changed his direction and began to ride east. Later in the afternoon he turned south, and as evening approached, the king and his court awaited the rider's return. He returned just as the sun was setting but the exhausted horse stumbled, throwing the man off its back and to the ground where he broke his neck. With the dead man stretched out at his feet the king turned to those around him and said, 'This man has won thousands of acres today and all he needs now is three by six'.

What is important? Is it wealth and property and power and privilege? Will these things, well nurtured in life, be truly important when all any of us needs is three by six? Or are there other things which are important and which get swallowed up and go without nurture, recognition or applause? Things like courage and hope, patience and gentleness, love well shared and laughter brought to others. What core things will we choose to nurture in this day and will they be important when all we need is three by six?

Wisdom in Weakness

Lesley Carroll

Life is not always kind to us. Sometimes we find ourselves involved in situations we would rather not be involved in or at the receiving end of circumstances which are beyond our control. And yet on reflection, in the years to come, or perhaps even in the process of living through difficult times, we can begin to understand kindness in a new way and be glad for what we can see in a new way.

Some of us are in a situation where we are dependent upon others. Unable to look after ourselves, unable to do the things we enjoy doing, unable to go out and make contact with others, we are dependent on people making contact with us. We are dependent upon others to remind us what living life is all about for we soon forget and our world becomes necessarily small. In those times, kind words are much appreciated. But if we pay attention, we will notice that there are many people who faithfully live beyond the kindness of words. They are the people who regularly pick up the telephone, who send a card or a note, who offer to do the shopping or who call from time to time to chat with us and to listen to us.

There is a deep wisdom that can come to us when we are vulnerable and feeling helpless. It is a gentle, understanding wisdom which is not tainted by judgement of other people categorising them into success and failure. It is, rather, wisdom given life by new seeing. It brings with it a new faith in human nature, a new appreciation of others and a new hope for the future. Often this wisdom comes from silent deeds done by others, from people who keep secret the good that they do. For these people, who grace our eyes with new seeing and our minds with new understanding, do not often flaunt the good that they do.

Such goodness is not recorded in newspaper headlines nor is it the stuff of which newsflashes are made. But it is the stuff of which life is made, real life. It is the stuff of all that is good and life-giving and full of hope and grace.

Once upon a time a man took some beautiful birds out of their cage. He then proceeded to kill them by crushing their heads. While he was doing this, it so happened that tears began to flow from his eyes. One of the birds left in the cage said to the others: 'Don't worry. Don't be afraid. I can see that he is weeping now and he will surely show us mercy and not kill us.' But the oldest bird replied: 'My son, do not look at his eyes; look at his hands.'

A New Lyric

Geraldine Smyth

Paul Robeson, the African-American singer, is remembered for his unrivalled bass voice that resonated in the deep caverns of the human soul, shaking the foundations of tone, feeling and rhythm. We remember him best, perhaps, for his rendering of 'Shenandoah' and 'Ol' Man River'.

In his early years as a singer, Robeson had become a standard-bearer for civil rights and the equality of African Americans. He was one of the first African Americans to graduate from an Ivy League university, combining in a magnificent persona the accomplishments of vocal artist and public speaker.

The Gershwin musicals established his reputation as a singer, and soon he became the voice of his people's long history of suffering and oppression. But, gradually, Robeson saw the need for the old self-understanding as slaves and victims to be transformed. Lyrics that reinforced the image of a passive or broken people were for him no longer adequate for folk with freedom on their minds and dignity in their hearts. The time had come to leave behind that old self-image of victimhood and passivity. After the long years of slavery, the conviction of being free and equal needed to be celebrated. Robeson persuaded Gershwin to let him adapt lyrics of the original Hammerstein song 'Ol' Man River': 'Ah gits weary/An' sick of tryin'!' to 'But I keeps laffin'/instead of cryin'!'. The old world-weary tones took on energy and joy. Robeson's songs reflected the new consciousness.[1]

'In a higher world it is otherwise,' wrote John Henry Newman, 'but here below to live is to change, and to be perfect is to have changed often.'[2] Few would doubt that our times demand change and the welcoming of diversity, as our world confronts the need for a new and different political culture, beyond state-centred interests or financial greed that results in violence and exploitation. We do need to imagine a different global order, expressed in new forms of trans-national cooperation, economic solidarity and intercultural respect. We all need to learn a new song – new words to challenge old images of siege and rebellion, of winner takes all and the weakest go to the wall; new songs of courage and capacity, new words of justice restored and diversities acknowledged. The psalms, those ancient songs of Jewish self-understanding that speak beyond the boundaries of national identity, give us a language to cry out, asking God to put a new song into our mouth; a song to carry us through the shudders of sectarian violence and injustice. New words to sustain the fragile confidence in ourselves as capable of peace and of living with difference.

1   Cf. 'Ol' Man River' on wikipedia.com, accessed 18.01.2010; cf. also 'Ol' Man River' in Will Friedwald, *Stardust Memories: The Biography of Twelve of America's Most Poplular Songs*, New York, Pantheon Books, 2002.

2   John Henry Newman, *An Essay on the Development of Doctrine*, London, Longmans, Green and Co., 1914 (1878), 40.

Promises to Keep

Geraldine Smyth

No society can survive without being able to rely on the word of another. Where one's word is no longer one's bond, trust fractures. Trust is never without risk, but it is a two-way street. Relationship cannot survive without reciprocity. Without give and take there will be little promise for 'a shared future'.

In my mother's last years, I used to visit her in a nursing home. Her body was frail and her mind was all but lost. Saying goodbye on one occasion, I tried to explain that I would be back the next day. I began wondering about the meaning of such a promise and whether it held any binding quality. She would not remember nor be disappointed if I failed to show up. And yet, I knew that such a promise was a bond between us: not to take it seriously would undermine her dignity and my integrity. To say, 'I will be here for you tomorrow', is to acknowledge that our lives are mysteriously interfused. To give or accept our word is to give our lives into each other's keeping. That is not to harbour illusions that we keep our word in every instance, but to recognise a feeling of being called to live up to our promises. To say, 'I will be here for you tomorrow' is to know that we touch a treasure that we cannot treat carelessly.

Such threads of faithfulness with those whose lives are implicated in ours remind us that we must listen for the underlying need or intent. In the making of promises, we weave connections between yesterday and today and tomorrow. I recently photographed a pavement stone in Edinburgh inscribed with John Buchan's words: 'We can only pay our debt to the past by putting the future in debt to us.' Promises hold the future open, paving a way between one generation and the next. To live without a promise is to keep quarrying the past for stones to obstruct the future. Eavan Boland, reflecting on the stories that both bind and transcend the generations, exclaims: 'Our children are our legends'. Turning to her daughter, she avows:

> And the world
> is less bitter to me
> because you will retell the story.[1]

At the Last Supper, in similar motherly tone, Jesus promises his friends not to leave them 'orphaned'. He gave himself as a pledge of a love that would survive his death, and hold true despite their betrayal or broken promises: 'If you love me you will keep my word ... Peace I leave with you' (Jn 14:15ff). This too is our story, and in retelling it for one another our world is healed of its bitterness.

1 Eavan Boland, 'Legends – for Eavan Frances', in In a Time of Violence, New York, W.W. Norton and Co., 1994, 50.

Moving Fences

Geraldine Smyth

Once, in a remote place in Eastern Europe, was settled a very traditional community – a community that had little contact with outsiders. Into their village came two missionaries whose simple mission was Christian work and witness, and helping anyone in need. Their ways were different, but over time the local people ceased regarding them as outsiders and came to trust them. Then a dreaded plague broke out and family after family was stricken. The two friends gave their days and nights to nursing the sick and consoling the bereaved. But just as the plague was easing, they too were struck down and died.

The villagers were distressed at the death of their friends, but were troubled about where to bury them. Their religious custom forbade the burial of those of different religious persuasion in the holy ground of their cemetery. The majority upheld the traditional practice. These people were their loyal friends, fellow Christians, who had laid down their life for them. But others thought this was not reason enough and wanted to stretch the rules. Eventually a 'compromise' was reached: they would be buried right beside the cemetery, but outside the perimeter fence. This was done, but few were satisfied with the convenient solution.

The following day, a young boy passed by and was amazed to find that the two graves had 'disappeared'. He ran and told the villagers. Sure enough, when the people arrived, no graves could be seen. And then it was discovered that the graves were now inside the cemetery. But how could this be? How could the graves that were outside yesterday be inside today? Who had moved the graves? There was a simple enough explanation. The graves were in the very same place, but during the night, in an act of stealth, someone had moved the fence.

Moving fences is sometimes a feat of daring, but always it requires imagination and a readiness to meddle. Identity is always formed in relationship, and it is always changing, always many-in-one. To keep investing energy in holding religious and cultural fences in place will maintain purity in the short-term – but disfigure God's gift of abundant life. I remember reading about some victims of the 1988 earthquake in Armenia who preferred to die rather than accept blood donations from Azerbaijanis, their historic enemies. Keeping the bloodlines uncontaminated was more important than living. Death by purity.

In the same vein, reflecting on the devastation of Rwanda and the supremacy of tribe over Christian faith, an African bishop once said to me, 'Blood is thicker than water, even the water of baptism'. And I thought of us here, where so many claim Christ as Lord, while bowing down before our own tribe and our own works, and refusing the grace of Christ, who has broken down the wall of hatred between us by his own life's blood (c.f. Eph 14–16).

Valiant Women

Lesley Carroll

Sojourner Truth was born into slavery in America. In 1852, while lecturing against slavery, she stopped in at a women's rights convention in Ohio. She cut a fine figure dressed in her plain grey dress and heads turned as she walked up the aisle of the church where the meeting was being held. She sat on the pulpit steps and listened as various speakers spoke out against women's rights. Sojourner Truth couldn't keep quiet for a moment longer.

She rose and climbed into the pulpit. She turned on those who said women were weak and needed help. She spoke of the fields she had ploughed and planted and of the crops she had gathered in. She spoke of the five children she had raised and then seen sold into slavery. She spoke of the depth of a mother's grief which no one but Jesus knew about. Soon the crowd began to applaud, boldly supporting her every word. All the silent, seemingly attentive crowd had needed was someone to speak out for them and Sojourner Truth had been courageous enough to do it. When she finally took her seat she did so to deafening applause.

How different Sojourner Truth's experience of life was to that of Queen Vashti. Her husband was a most powerful ruler. He had expensive tastes and money to satisfy them. Vashti shared in his wealth and power and threw her own banquets. The king loved to show off his beautiful queen and so, after a week of over-indulgence, he sent for Vashti. The unutterable, unthinkable happened. Vashti took control over her own life and refused to appear. Vashti refused to be exploited. The king was livid. Not only had Vashti disobeyed him, she had shown him up in front of his friends. Vashti was never heard of again and the king began the process of choosing a new queen.

Vashti and Sojourner Truth were women of vastly different backgrounds but they both held their dignity and they both stood by their convictions. Their stories have encouraged others to live lives faithful to themselves, to have the courage not to compromise in the face of belittling behaviour. They remind us that our courage can be the stepping stone for someone else to stand on their own dignity. God created us all in God's own image. No one is any better that the other and no one has the right to demean others. In God's image we all have our dignity and importance.

Cherishing Children

Lesley Carroll

David Bailie Warden was born towards the end of the eighteenth century near to Greyabbey on the Ards peninsula. He was the eldest son of three, his father a farmer. It was the hope of David's parents that he would grow up to be a Presbyterian minister, but when they discussed the matter with his school teacher they found no encouragement, for they were told that David would never make anything but a blockhead.

It is surprising then to discover how this child grew into a man who studied at university in Glasgow and there obtained a Master of Arts degree, having received prizes along the way. His politics were not unlike many of his day for he was an ardent United Irishman, and for his leanings he found himself in jail in Downpatrick. From there he was placed on a prison ship, living in a crowded space of not more than four feet eight inches high. Dr William Steel Dickson recorded the scene: the lack of space, the dank and scarce air and the way in which a young man, David Bailie Warden, kept them in lively, interesting and challenging conversation.

After six weeks David was returned to Downpatrick jail, where he was eventually released on his agreement to emigrate to America for good. There he taught and continued with his studies until he received his degree of Doctor of Medicine. He was later appointed Consul-General of the United States in Paris, where he was to end his days thirty-eight years later, having published various celebrated works and belonged to a number of academically respectable societies. He never returned to his own country, to the place where it had been predicted that he would be nothing but a blockhead.

In the book of Proverbs we read that even a child knows what he is by what he does. In this instance it was well that David Bailie Warden, the child, knew better what he was than his own teacher. People with influence over the young can make or break their confidence; pull down or build up their vision; hold back their enthusiasm or encourage them in their plans, hopes and dreams. To have the care of children, in whatever way, is a great responsibility. The writer of Psalm 127 says, 'Children are a gift from the Lord, they are a real blessing.' Whether or not David Bailie Warden knew that he was a gift from the Lord in those childhood years is debatable, but what better way to ground a child's life than in the knowledge that they are a gift from God? As precious gifts are cherished and given space, so too our children should be cherished and given space for they are more than any other precious gift; they are a gift from the Lord.

Lifelines

Lesley Carroll

Faithful friends can be hard to find; friends who will stand by us no matter what. Sometimes we are disappointed. We live out our part in the unspoken deal by making ourselves available, by giving our time and energy, by offering a listening ear and by giving back challenge when we think that is what is needed. We don't offer friendship solely because of what we can get out of it, but I suppose we might all have to admit to an element of self-interest. When life hits a wall and we need our friends, then we become more aware of that self-interest as we expect those whom we have befriended to be there for us. We hope that we will find a lifeline; our friendship reciprocated. But friendship isn't easy; it takes time and energy.

Naomi had gone with her husband and sons to live in a strange country. They had hoped to find happiness, and indeed Naomi's sons had married and settled down. But the story is tainted with sadness and tragedy, for in that strange country Naomi's husband and sons died, leaving her feeling very alone and longing to return to her home and the family and friends she had left behind.

Naomi told her daughters-in-law that she intended to return to her home and she freed them of worry about her, telling them they could stay in their own home country. She managed to persuade one daughter-in-law to stay but the other one, Ruth, couldn't be persuaded. She had come to care for Naomi. She was family and friend and Ruth wanted to stay with her even at tremendous cost to herself. So Ruth left home and travelled with Naomi. She wasn't afraid of choosing the way which would make her vulnerable.

In friendship such demanding measures are seldom called for but openness to vulnerability is real in every friendship. We open ourselves to the possibility of being let down but we also open ourselves to the tremendous joy that comes from the authentic company of others.

Our experience of friendship in the past can affect how, or even if, we form friendships in the future. Fear and bitterness can keep us from forming new friendships. But we have a choice – the choice to risk it all again, forgiving those who have let us down, and moving on in search of company. Or we can choose to deny ourselves friendship for fear of being hurt all over again. It may also be true that we need to forgive ourselves in order to move on, forgive ourselves for how we have let others down.

Trust

Geraldine Smyth

'I wouldn't trust him as far as I'd throw him.' Those words bear the sentiments of an old neighbour – one of those archetypes that endure in the landscape of memory, so aptly described by John Montague as 'dolmens round my childhood'.[1] Trust has an Anglo-Saxon clip to it, though its hard sounds hedge a softer core, with meanings of mutual understanding, integrity and faithful duty. The same double edge is found in its twin word – tryst. A 'tryst' hints at secret meetings of lovers. But in more prosaic terms it means a cattle fair. However brutish that sounds, a cattle fair is not without its own romance. It depends upon such reliabilities as turning up at the agreed spot; keeping a balance between credulity in the other's claims about the seed, breed and generation and one's own judgement of the state and gait of the beast in question. Folk at a mart must be familiar with its lore – at ease in the rhetoric of the few words; the know-how of reading inscrutable signals in the gaze of buyer or seller; expert in intuition of the exact moment when the deal is sealed by the spit on the hand. Trysting places are betimes places of risk and folly. Jack went to the market with a cow and came home with a future beanstalk. More a robbery than fair exchange, at first glance, and his mother blamed his trust on naive gullibility! But who got the better deal? In the end, the deception played on Jack did not prevent their prosperity and transformation.

We read in the Bible that there is nothing more devious than the human heart, but also that trust overcomes distrust. 'I wouldn't trust them as far as I'd throw them', was not the attitude of Jesus, whether in his encounter with the Samaritan woman, the tax-collector, or brigand on the cross. To follow Jesus is to trust his promise of peace beyond the ways of the world and his invitation to the table of justice where those with right and title are deposed in favour of outsiders. Here today, are we prepared to give over our codes and covers, and risk plain dealing and honest cooperation – as politicians, churches, citizens? Do we dare trust in the Spirit who never ceases to tryst with us, and through whom what was hidden will be brought to light, and things once spoken in whispers will be proclaimed from the housetops (Lk 8:17)?

1   From *Collected Poems of John Montague*, Oldcastle, Gallery Books, 1995, 12–13.

Providence

Geraldine Smyth

One feature of life today is a preoccupation with pensions. Pension company advertisements compete in promising bigger slices of their giant cherry-crowned cakes. As we baby-boomers square up to retirement, just like the markets we are jittery and nervous as stocks take a tumble into the murky waters of corporate scandals and scams on an untold scale. Governments admonish us to adjust our expectations of lump sums and guaranteed payments. Few stop to think that in the virtual world of non-accountable global trillions, there are billions of impoverished people whose lives are un-distracted by stocks because they have no shares, no stake in this brave new world. All are supposed to find security within the iron laws of the system.

In the film *About Schmidt*, Jack Nicholson plays a formulaic 'everyman' whose grey life is determined by the system: going to work, earning and saving, coming home to a jaded marriage. And then the displacement of being retired: each day bringing more of the same – always taking stock, and never taking risks.

The sudden death of his wife sets him adrift and unhinges his whole sense of self. Eventually, he stocks up the camper van and sets off. For all the mock-heroic overtones of Homer's *Odyssey*, the aim of his journey is to find his daughter and persuade her to come home with him and keep house. But he does attain glimpses of self-discovery, as the banalities of his half-lived life are prised loose. Then he is catapulted into his daughter's groovy lifestyle (Kathy Bates presiding magnificently over the crazy collection of hippy in-laws, with their passion and unpredictability and madly sane ideals). Schmidt is paralysed by it all – fearing that if he loses his cool or gives offence, the carefully constructed walls of his life will fall apart, leaving him like some ancient Humpty Dumpty. But in fact, this eccentric, vibrant world reminds him that he is still alive. His self-securities laid bare, the driven persona begins to dissolve, and he feels the pain of not having loved anyone for a very long time … All very middle-class, self-indulgent Hollywood, no doubt.

Yet there is a parable in there about a time for taking stock and a time for taking risks. Wisdom is found somewhere in the gaps, in trusting to a Providence that shapes our ends, rough-hew them though we will. Today, that gracious Providence calls us to be its human face – to have a care for others, to be a little reckless with our own sum of securities, in solidarity with those whose very life really is at risk in our runaway world.

Words

Geraldine Smyth

'For words alone are certain good,' said W.B. Yeats.[1] I like to poke at words, lift up the stones lying on top of them to see what is lurking or scuttling underneath. At other times I just take pleasure in them, dwell on them and let their sound and sense swirl around inside, stirring up memories – and imagination. Words provide passageways into our soul, build bridges into the minds of others, or even open a door on the Spirit of God. 'To my words give ear O God, let my prayer come before you,' said the Psalmist (Ps 5:1).

A word is its own passport into the other times and places which it has travelled through the centuries. How odd, some of the everyday words of our grandparents – quaint, awkward and embarrassing at times. Those were days when parents 'fetched up' their children; when men went out to turn the sod, while womenfolk 'red up' the kitchen, and we were told not to 'cast a clout' – and I thought that meant not to be clodding stones! All those Anglo-Saxon words, not just the four letter ones – short, sharp, gutsy, or worn at the edges by local accent, alive in the tongue of common statement, giving texture to the warp and woof of everyday life: work, lift, heft, drouth, shift, fornenst.

Seamus Heaney speaks of our 'word-hoard',[2] and indeed such speech is a kind of treasure, inherited or robbed from here, there and yonder; spoils after a raid or battle, the bittersweet fruit of invaders and settlers, in the colonising ways of history. Words could defeat each other, or join forces in hybrid vigour of foreign and familiar idiom of landowner or serf.

After the Norman invasion, the coarser Anglo-Saxon words stood their ground in the speech of herdsmen and shepherds. The natives who tended the animals called them by their old names – pig, cow, sheep, deer. But when the same animals were served on salvers up at the manor, the names were Frenchified in civilized syllables. In refined dining rooms a pig turned into pork. People ate beef, not Daisybell the cow. In these nicer circles, sheep became mutton, while the deer leaping around until felled in last week's hunt attained the solemn status of venison.

Words are human companions. We can shelter behind them, or offer them in token of praise and thanks. Language is the trusted currency of our human loves and of our whispered prayers. But what brings words alive is the act of listening, and listening needs a receptive space of inner quiet. Today, as we listen in to the old words of collective speech, and listen out for the new ones, we stop and give them space to echo in us. We take heed of T.S. Eliot's chiding:

> *Where shall the word be found, where will the Word Resound? Not here. There is not enough silence ...*[3]

1   'The Song of the Happy Shepherd', in *Collected Poems*, Macmillan and Co., London, 1934 (1933), 7–8, 8.
2   'North', in *Opened Ground: Selected Poems, 1966–1996*, London, Faber and Faber, 100–101, 101.
3   'Ash Wednesday', op. cit., 89–99, 96.

The Good That We Do

Lesley Carroll

Atlanta, Georgia – what a wonderful city to visit. I can recommend it, despite the heat, and despite the difficulties I experienced getting in and out of MARTA, the underground system, which efficiently takes you from one place to another, if you can find your way in and out of it. This was my shortcoming, of course, for it didn't work like the London Underground. Atlanta is the home of Coca Cola and the headquarters of Habitat for Humanity. It is the place where Martin Luther King ministered and where a number of impressive museums can be visited to enable the visitor to begin to understand the world King lived in and what drove his commitment. There is sight after sight and place of interest after place of interest.

Margaret Mitchell, the writer of *Gone with the Wind*, was born and lived in Atlanta, Georgia. The house dedicated to her memory is large and beautiful, filled with pictures of her family and friends, recounting her life's story. She and her husband, however, did not live in this magnificent house but in a few small rooms at the back of it – rooms that they rented for the duration of their lives. It was in one of those small rooms that she sat to pen her famous novel. She didn't write it to bring pleasure to the world but to entertain herself when she was unable to move around freely. Little did she know, as she passed those hours of immobility, that her words would one day be published and sell so well. *Gone with the Wind* has sold in numbers second only to the Bible.

The Atlanta of Margaret Mitchell's day was a divided city. Blacks and whites did not mix freely and if, by chance, there was any mixing, there was often uproar. Mitchell, however, decided to support black students in their studies.

Many of them did not discover until years later who their benefactor had been for Margaret chose not to tell of her good deeds. Surely this is exactly what the biblical principle of not letting your right hand know what your left hand is doing is actually all about.

For Jesus, the principle was about the good that we do: 'Beware of practising your piety before others in order to be seen by them; for then you have no reward from your Father in heaven' (Mt 6:1).

To love and not to desire love in return. To give, without seeking any reward for ourselves. To give without knowing that there will be a return for us. There are always ways to be found which fulfil God's command to us to love one another as God has loved us. It is possible for us to practise our piety before others in order for others to see it but it is more important to do as Margaret Mitchell did and do the good we choose to do simply because it is God's way, the way of God's kingdom.

Night Lights

Lesley Carroll

I remember the very first time I really looked at the stars. It was for a school project. We had learnt about the Plough, Orion and the Little Bear and we were sent home with instructions to look at the stars that night and note their different colours and brightness. I had always thought of the stars as being yellow and had crayoned them in as such in my pictures. When darkness had set in, and the frosty night allowed me to glimpse the immensity of the universe, I went outside to peer into the sky. As I looked, very carefully, I was amazed to see green and blue and red and orange. I looked again, incredulous, and saw each star as individually bright and individually beautiful and joining with the other stars to brighten the night sky. I confess to being so amazed that I looked up an encyclopaedia when I came inside, just to check that I hadn't been seeing things.

In his letter to the Church at Philippi, Paul urges the Christians there to keep on living lives which shine like lights in the night sky. Each one with their own individuality, beauty and creativity adds to the brightness, joining in one shining light. Their light joins his, and his light join theirs, for in this family of God everyone has a place and we don't all have to be the same.

> So then, dear friends, as you always obeyed me when I was with you, it is even more important that you obey me now while I am away from you. Keep on working with fear and trembling to complete your salvation, because God is always at work in you to make you willing and able to obey his own purpose.

Do everything without complaining or arguing, so
that you may by innocent and pure as God's perfect
children in a world of corrupt and sinful people.
You must shine among them as stars lighting up
the sky, as you offer them the message of life.
(Phil 2:12-15)

It is a bold vision of how the community of God's people
should live in God's world. Each of us has to find our
own way, our own colour and shape. Each of us finds
ourselves within different constellations yet situated within
the broader sky of stars. Each of us, in our own place, is to
live as a star lighting up the sky, the message of our lives
providing the shape and colour of our witness.

So as each new morning dawns, we, the people of God,
proclaim that the night is ended and the stars shine in colour
and brightness in other places. The night is ended, but the
light of our lives rises on our part of the world today. We
rejoice in our difference, our variety, our individuality. We
celebrate our unity, our one shining light, offering glory to
God who is the light of the world.

Alive

Lesley Carroll

'My name is Lester Burnham. This is my neighbourhood. This is my street. This is my life. I'm forty-two years old. In less than a year I'll be dead. Of course, I don't know that yet. And in a way, I'm dead already.'

These depressing words mark the beginning of the acclaimed movie *American Beauty*. The tone is set for the next couple of hours – cynical, depressing and verging, at times, on the abusive. The story takes place in an ordinary North American neighbourhood and focuses on two families who, to all intents and purposes, seem quite normal. Parents with quite normal livelihoods and the usual angry teenagers boasting about achievements never made and keeping secret interests that please them.

But the film exposes the veneer that surrounds the lives of these ordinary families. Rituals lived out to suppress sexuality, honesty and fear. The greatest fear, it would seem, is to crack the veneer, for it holds things together in an almost unethical, yet precise, balance. Balance it is, even if it does conceal all sorts of dysfunctional behaviour and thinking. I suppose one of the most pleasing aspects of this movie for me is that it does not blame youth culture entirely for all its own dysfunctions – adults don't escape the critical eye of the narrator either.

In this last year of his life the hero of the hour, Lester Burnham, actually discovers how to live. It is he who cracks the veneer just enough to tip the balance and bring the film to a crescendo of violent, cynical, almost hysterical behaviour, and hence to its conclusion.

It gives nothing away to tell you that Lester Burnham loses his life, for you will have known that since the very beginning of the film. This is, of course, the great irony of it all – discovering life leads to the end of life. The paradoxical twist in the tale reveals a pessimism that is hard to take. But it may be that this darkness, this sarcastic, scornful, sceptical swipe at life and its values, are actually what pervade society. And if it doesn't pervade society then it almost certainly threatens it.

Odd then that the gospel says that life is found through losing it. The Bible tells us:

> You were dead through the trespasses and sins in which you once lived ... But God, who is rich in mercy, out of the great love with which he loved us even when we were dead through our trespasses, made us alive together with Christ ... (Col 2:13)

Let's Talk

Geraldine Smyth

It's good to talk, as the slogan tells us. But in truth, good conversation is hard to come by. Now, that is not a tongue-in-cheek remark about our slowness of speech with those we view as 'opposite' to ourselves. Nor is it a dig at our characteristic Northern resistance to face-to-face talks. Though in recent times, our greater ease with hurling stones than with weaving words into a loose net of connection cannot be disputed. And even today, it is strange how some of our political leaders will parley and do business behind closed doors, but do not like to be seen talking with certain others.

Theodore Zeldin, rated among the top forty world figures whose ideas are reckoned to make a lasting impact in this millennium, views conversation as 'the meetings on the borderline of what I understand with people who are different from myself'.[1] So, he urges the need of conversation, in places where there are clashes of belief. Just imagine the critical conversation that might have averted Crusades or the Holocaust; the difference made by the apt word in the right place, by ears hearkening to the words, to the feelings behind the words, and the silence between the words. But conversation has a closer connection to religion than fighting over creeds.

Conversation itself is a religious act. Conversation and conversion have the same root meaning, suggesting turning around and turning towards. After an authentic conversation we will never be the same again. I imagine God as the first great conversationalist, the One inclining and listening for the first whisper of a word from us, One who is at ease with the silence in the spaces between.

The old English word 'gossip' originally had God in the middle of it – 'God-sib'. But somewhere along the road the word was emptied of that divine core. It used to mean a sponsor at baptism, someone spiritually related, your divine sibling – sib in God. In the word and image of gossip, there are undertones of gospel, of spreading good news. It was women who were the first 'God-sibs', proclaiming that Jesus was risen and alive. The disbelieving apostles accused them of 'empty gossip'. Christ is known as the Word of God – the *Dei Verbum*. Through Christ, we see that God is not a noun, but a verb – the doing-word of God, the doing-word in the sentences that make of our lives a conversation.

1   From *Converstaion: How Talk Can Change Our Lives*, New York, Hidden Spring, 2000 (1998), p. 88.

Home and Away

Geraldine Smyth

Holidays are as old as the hills. Travel to faraway places. High Days and Holy Days. Doing things differently. Time out. Visits to distant relatives; cousins home from Canada, enjoying the craic, anxious not to wear out their welcome. Opportunities for young people to come and go in foreign countries, finding a home with strangers.

Part of us is fascinated by the exotic and foreign. On holidays we seek out something unique to bring back home – something that wee bit odd and out of the ordinary. We fill the familiar corners of our houses with haphazard bits of pottery, plates that hang, strange-looking spoons, lamps that began their lives as bottles or giant seashells. A far cry from sticky rocks from Bundoran or a souvenir lighthouse from Donaghadee.

We have cultivated new tastes in food and dress, formed surprising friendships, expanded our outlook and language to include people and worlds other than our own. Inside us are new songs, unsuspected dances, because of holidays. Because we decided to cross the water, cross borders, our identity has been deepened and changed. We have been enriched by the giving and receiving of gifts, but influenced also by the moments of panic when we could neither understand nor be understood; the uneasy experience of feeling far away from anything familiar; the need to depend on someone to interpret or act as guide.

W.R. Rodgers writes of this kind of self-discovery:

> Strange that, in lands, and countries quite unknown,
> We find, not other's strangeness, but our own;
> That is one use of journeys; if one delves,
> Differently, one's sure to find one's selves.[1]

In Ireland, north and south, and indeed in our increasingly cosmopolitan world, we are discovering our identities as fluid, not fixed; overlapping, many-in-one. Like Ruth, our foremother in the faith, we are called to journey beyond our first identity and tradition, to discover new faces of ourselves in the face of the Other. In this strange place we call home, where so many of us are estranged from one another and strangers to ourselves, the words of Ruth come to us across the distance as a hard saying and a faint hope:

> Where you go, I will go;
> Where you lodge, I will lodge;
> your people shall be my people,
> and your God, my God. (Ruth 1:16-17)

1 'The Journey of the Magi', in *W.R. Rodgers: Collected Poems* (Michael Longley, ed.), Oldcastle, Gallery Press, 1969, 56–63, 60–61.

What Are We Communicating?

Geraldine Smyth

Ours is the communication age extraordinaire. The text reigns, iPads and iPods keep us wired for business and leisure. Disconnection is hell. I text, therefore I am. *iPhone ergo sum*. And yet, often where people talk up the life of communications, the less communication we witness in actual lives.

In places where sectarianism or racism rule, folk can be suspicious of much speech. We are selective in our conversation partners, downsizing life's diversities to slogans, its subtle dilemmas to dogmas. Scottish poet, Iain Crichton Smith, writing in the impassioned style of Robert Burns, suggests that refusal of communication renders life cheap and inhuman. He could be addressing us directly:

> ... there leap across your local walls
>   blood-red ideas
> of kin and creed, to smash a door.
> Members of an élitest corps
> you tear at the colourful décor
>   that men must build
> to identify that they are here,
> by self beguiled.[1]

With the recurrence of violent incidents in Ireland, whether politically or gangland motivated, or targeted against migrant workers, the picture is chilling and familiar. But besides the relentless parade of brutal images, the poet also offers fleeting, saving glimpses of an alternative human harmony, pointing to: 'Life's various and bright discourses'

– the 'natural harmonies and dissonances' of the local landscapes; the human rhythm of 'births and funerals and dances' or, what he terms, 'the changing scene / of this our home'. Why not, he urges,

> create our music and our art,
> O not dogmatic but a sort
> of praise, or ladder from the heart
> emphatic, glorious:
> at humanity's multifarious court
> narrate our stories, ...[2]

Narrating stories – of who we are and of the desires of our hearts, sharing the bread of justice with strangers – is the Spirit's alternative to nailing our identity to flag, territory or turf. Exploiting the rhetoric of our rights, and ring-binding our losses into folders on the subject of single-identity cripples the hope of our own and others' flourishing. Zygmunt Bauman warns of the addictive nature of identity politics: '[A] battlefield is identity's natural home,' he says. Yet, paradoxically, 'Identity comes to life only in the tumult of battle; it falls asleep and silent the moment the noise of the battle dies down.'[3] Eucharist is Christ's alternative to 'the tumult of battle'; holy communion the spiritual alternative to devouring or being devoured; an invitation to communicate truthfully about the space we share and the future we would pledge to our children.

1   Iain Crichton Smith, *The Human Face*, Manchester, Carcanet Press, 1996, 7–8.
2   Ibid., 66.
3   Zygmunt Bauman, *Identity*, Cambridge, Polity Press, 2004, 77.

The Man

Lesley Carroll

The man lived in rooms at the back of the Lodge where we stayed on our holidays. Up early, dressed in t-shirts and shorts and wellies (the order of the day on such holidays), we would make our way, bent double, to the low window of the man's living room to wait and watch for him getting up. He was something of a fascination to us. Our hearts beat hard and loud as we waited, and morning after morning we were rewarded by the sight of the Man walking into the living room, kilt and shirt as dishevelled as his hair, scratching and yawning, with his wee Jack Russell terriers, Patch and Kirsty, jumping around his legs.

Morning after morning my mother or aunt would come out and whisper in reprimanding tones – come away, what are yis doing anyway! We're watching the Man, was always our reply. He went out at nights and returned home late. We were never sure how he got back because these holidays were spent far from civilization – we drove to remote and then drove on for at least another hour before we reached the isolated, peaceful, wonderful place.

The Man was what is known as a stalker, not in the sense that we use the word most commonly. He helped those who wanted to stalk and shoot deer, and he helped as a gilly on the estate – a valued employee who knew his work well. He had family from whom he had parted but who visited regularly and became part of the circle of friends we developed on our regular holidays. The Man had been a brave commando, we knew – rugged and fit, serving his country well and learning the disciplines of life which stood by him in his remote surroundings and often lonely work.

We never knew nor asked what had happened to separate him from his family, but we made our guesses, learning from our watching that night clothes and day clothes were interchangeable for the Man, as he returned in the early hours and awoke with a sore head and a short temper. Perhaps these days we are less content to take people as we find them and need to know more of their background and circumstances. How easily we forget that we don't need to know everything, for the one who created the world and everything in it knows and sees all things and all people.

The Psalmist expresses it best: my frame was not hidden from you, when I was made in the secret place. When I was woven together in the depths of the earth, your eyes saw my unformed body. All the days ordained for me were written in your book before one of them came to be (Ps 139:15-16).

As God knows all things, perhaps we should be content to know less and to take people as we find them.

Kilty's Home

Lesley Carroll

Kilty lived in a bothy beside the burn. I have never had a bothy properly defined for me, but this place was ramshackle and wooden, with dark smoke snaking into the sky from a makeshift chimney; a place he never entered. It didn't have running water as far as we knew, and in our childish minds we had all sorts of ideas as to what the bothy looked like inside.

These childish imaginings were fed by the stories the adults told. Kilty was something of an oddity, an eccentric, what we carefully call a 'character'. No one knew where he had come from. He had simply turned up one day, either towards the end of World War II or shortly after it, and he had been wearing a kilt. Hence his name – Kilty – a name we were never allowed to call him to his face and a name we only seldom heard an adult let slip in his company. But Kilty was no mug – he was clearly well read, and stories abounded of a library, housed in the bothy, a library of rare and valuable books which Kilty shared with no one. And on days when we all got a little carried away, the valuable books were watched over by valuable paintings and who knew what else of value.

When we were children we were a little in awe of him. So when he returned from work in the evening the word would go around the house, 'Kilty's home'. Or when evening came and the fishermen returned burdened with the catch of the day and I was sent to the scullery to begin gutting the fish, Kilty would inevitably make his way across the yard in his plus-4s and deerstalker, put his head through the window and inquire if it had been the kind of day when the fish liked to rise near the surface and unwittingly grasp the hand-tied fly.

Kilty has since passed on and the contents of the bothy were divided among those who were brave enough and compassionate enough to give him a welcome into their lives and to care for him as his health failed. He had found and created family for himself in that small highland community. The stories remain of the man who came from who knows where, grew up with people of whom he never spoke and was thrust into that small community by circumstances completely unknown. His story reminds us of the words of Jesus as he points to those who will be welcome in the coming Kingdom – I was a stranger and you welcomed me in.

Stepping Out

Lesley Carroll

I was sitting in a church recently looking at the intricate and beautiful stained-glass window in front of me. It is somewhat unpresbyterian, not our usual style, and was placed in memory of the sixty-two members of the congregation who were killed in the blitz on Belfast in 1941. What is going to happen to it, I wondered? The building I was sitting in is to be closed and the congregation will move to worship on the site where I now work. We are going through all the thinking and planning and grieving and hoping that goes with closing a beloved place of worship and beginning something new. Our commitment is to making one new congregation, and to do that we need to represent both congregations in the shared place of worship, and from that symbolism of the past, the symbolism of two congregations, build one new congregation. It would be wonderful to bring that window not only because it is beautiful but because it represents a history of courage and commitment, a history of adventuring out from adversity back into God's world again. That is a history worth retaining.

It is a history reminiscent of the journey Abraham made with his family and a few possessions, a journey out into the unknown but a journey on which the people were assured that God would be with them. Know that I am with you and will keep you wherever you go, was a promise that God made time and again to adventuring people prepared to get up and risk and go on. It is a promise that God still makes to adventuring people who, in faith, step up and step out from their adversity, not in denial of it but confronting it with a faith that believes the most important thing of all is that God will be present.

God will be present in our individual choices for new things – moving to a new place for a new job; moving to university; moving to a new home, perhaps in a new relationship; shifting our political allegiance or changing our opinion; meeting with our 'enemies'. All our journeys into the unknown make us adventurers, like Abraham, who have to admit that at times we are afraid to leave behind the familiar things. But those familiar things often keep us from experiencing the truth of God's promise to be with us wherever we go. The God of adventurers gives us the courage we need to step up and step out in Abrahamic faith.

Hope from Trees

Geraldine Smyth

I live near an old monastic ruin associated with St Maelruain, an eighth century monk. There is a Dominican Priory and parish there now and on the grounds is a walled garden. In the garden is Maelruain's tree. It is a walnut tree, hundreds of years old, and records tell us that until 1797 the main trunk stood five feet tall. At that time it then sundered down the middle, its branches spreading over the ground. Nowadays, its divided boughs, especially in winter or in moonlight, look bent and gaunt as if stricken once and for all in some great lightning storm. And yet year by year the old tree puts out buds and continues to bear walnuts, still giving shelter to birds and animals; standing like a sentinel or bearing witness like Lear on the heath to some mighty calamity, recalling the avowal that 'the oldest have borne most', and that in God's great purpose, our triumphs and defeats are small matters and even the most ancient rivalries can spend themselves.

Of late, two veteran political leaders, Ian Paisley and Bertie Ahern, have retired from the centre-stage of Irish politics. On several occasions in recent years, they had come from either end of our divided island and in bold gesture set ancient enmities aside. I recall especially their meeting on the site of the Battle of the Boyne on the occasion of the opening of a multi-million euro heritage centre. For more than three hundred years the place and the name of the Boyne has been synonymous with our contested and divisive history. In a bold imagining, the reality was borne home that more of our past than we have often cared to admit is full of shared experiences, marked by the human bonds of suffering and celebration as well as by boundaries and borders. And so the Boyne site was commissioned, so to speak, as belonging not to one tradition alone, and its future held a promise of both traditions finding a place there. Dr Paisley presented a long decommissioned musket to Mr Ahern, recalling that a short time before in St Andrew's with its renewed terms of agreement, the man from Dublin had presented the man from Ballymena with a gift of a wooden bowl carved from a walnut tree that had fallen on the site of the Boyne. This was to mark the bond of fifty years of marriage being celebrated by Ian and Eileen Paisley – a reminder of the interplay of the personal and the political and the intertwining of the fidelities and hopes that make up our lives.

So, I thank God for walnut bowls betokening living fidelity and hope, for decommissioned muskets and for all those who have chanced their arm for peace. I praise God for all those who, like Maelruain's doughty walnut tree, have suffered hard and long, split apart but still sending down roots into the soil of God's ever-renewed creation, still bearing fruit in due season, still full of sap, still green (Ps 92:14).

'I Don't Want to Talk About It'

Geraldine Smyth

I remember enjoying a film some time back from the Latin American director, María Luisa Bemberg. The English title was I Don't Want to Talk About It. It portrayed a child, later a young woman, who had been born with the condition we know as dwarfism. She was quite at home with herself, talented, an accomplished performer, and eager to learn about the exotic world beyond the confines of her small Argentine town. Not so her mother, whose way of coping with her daughter's differentness was to deny it totally. Not only did she refuse to talk about it, but she went to absurd lengths to prevent her daughter from seeing herself as short, or facing anything that might reflect back her smallness. By stealth of night the mother smashed up a neighbour's garden dwarfs; a bonfire was made of all books with heroes like Gulliver, Thumbelina, Tom Thumb. Snow White and her seven friends were quite unmentionable.

We might not go to the same lengths, but most of us find it difficult to live with difference. Avoidance, rejection, embarrassment are some of our responses. Another is to view the person or group as the source of trouble, to separate ourselves, form ghettoes, or try to get rid of 'them'. In some cultures, a child born with a disfigurement is left out to die, or such a one may be regarded as blessed with special powers and exploited to advantage. We are familiar with the powerful idea of the scapegoat – selected to bear the sins of the group and driven out into the wilderness (Lev 16:20-22). That logic is deeply ingrained in us. Rather than recognise chaos and difference as part of the natural scheme of things, we move to suppress unruly forces, impose order, tame diversity. We seek self-security by doing anything with difference rather than accept it. Deny, overcompensate, demonize, eliminate. We convince ourselves that we are normal, good, wholly decent, by projecting what we don't like in ourselves, or what it is we most fear, onto those who are different. We put them beyond the pale and judge ourselves righteous. For the poet, on the other hand, difference spells contrast and tension, creativity, spells surprise and possibility. Gerard Manley Hopkins glorified God for whatever was fickle or freckled, spare or strange.[1] Another poet, Louis MacNeice, rejoiced likewise in life as 'incorrigibly plural' and celebrated the 'drunkenness of things being various'.[2]

So it was with Jesus Christ. His way was neither to pretend that differences did not exist, nor to reject those deemed as 'different'. In a world where conformity was all, where religious leaders prided themselves on ethnic purity, and enslaved others to legal systems, Jesus mingled with tax-collectors and prostitutes and dined out with pagans. He made himself beholden to the Samaritan woman by asking her for a drink. Jesus praised the tenth leper, the foreigner and the only one who returned to give thanks. Mark's gospel tells repeatedly of his crossing over to 'the other side of the lake' (Mk 6:45ff). So much did Jesus identify with the outsider that he took their rejection onto himself and was crucified between two felons outside the city walls (Lk 23:32-33). To live in the new life of Christ is to go out and proclaim this good news to all and sundry, unless, like the mother in the film, we can't accept it and we 'don't want to talk about it'.

1 See 'Pied Beauty', in Selected Poems (James Reeves, ed.), London, Heinemann, 1967 (1953), 24.
2 'Snow', in Louis MacNeice: Selected Poems (Michael Longley, ed.), London, Faber and Faber, 1988, 23.

There's Room for Roses

Geraldine Smyth

My niece Donna loves trees. One May morning back in
1974, we walked together up the Serpentine Road in North
Belfast. Donna was four. She repeated after me the names
of the trees we passed: rose, lilac, magnolia, rhododendron.
That last one was tricky, but Donna delighted in this naming
game as we went on our way. Another bright morning some
weeks later drew us out for a walk. Can you remember this
one? Rose, that's right. And this, and this? Magnolia. Rho-
do-dendron – harder to pronounce. And this? The small
brow furrowed – and then I realised that the blossoms had
vanished in the passing weeks, giving room to more green
leaves. It's the lilac, Donna, lilac, but the flowers have died.
Her face clouded: 'Who shot them?'

Many times through the years of the Troubles, that
question returned with its look of confusion and pain. Who
shot the lilacs? How had death come to be associated in
the child's mind with violence and murder? There, on that
morning under Cave Hill, in fairly quiet streets sweeping
down to Belfast Lough? Innocence and even nature tainted?

Some years later, still with no end to the violence
in prospect, I drove two Swiss visitors around Belfast,
wanting to quell their anticipated questions and more so
the predictable answers that would seek to make sense of
so many years and lives largely wasted. At one point we
were driving in and around the peace-line, and I found
myself naming names and recalling events. Bombay Street
– burnout; Lanark Way – intimidations; Springfield Road
Methodist Church – arson attacks. Walls and divisions once
on the streets, embedded now in the memory and etched
on faces. Just at the point of becoming morose, we found
ourselves caught up in a different kind of mid-street battle

– a seven-aside football postscript to a recent round of the World Cup. Suddenly cheered by this irrepressible display of carefree childhood, we continued through the streets of those hastily built small houses aproned with non-descript gardens. Then, a catch of breath as we noticed in the greyness a single house and garden coming down with rose trees – tumbles of them in what seemed a hundred shades of defiant pink. 'Yes,' Heidi declared, 'in the middle of all this, there's room for roses!'

Sharing Burdens

Lesley Carroll

The area where I live in North Belfast has long been known as a patchwork of Protestant and Catholic communities, or more properly of Unionist and Nationalist communities – small segments of streets interfacing with one another. Often the territory is contested, one group trying to add it to their community while the other fears its loss. That loss threatens a community's sense of stability and its view of itself. Living in Northern Ireland we have all sorts of fixations that people in other places don't have. We reflect regularly on the shifts and changes in population. Streets once populated by Protestants are now populated by Catholics. Streets with kerbstones painted green, white and gold are now painted red, white and blue. We bemoan our losses, seeing them as gain for the other side, and despair of the future.

North Belfast's New Lodge Road, once populated by Protestants from the Unionist tradition, is now, to the best of my knowledge, populated only by Catholics Nationalists. The story could be repeated all over Northern Ireland, with each side focusing on what has been lost. You can imagine my surprise when, driving up the New Lodge Road, I was greeted by two famous Presbyterians. Of Protestant faith and Protestant lineage they were there in all their glory for all to see – Mary Ann and Henry Joy McCracken.

Their memories are enshrined on a wall. Of United Irish commitment they may have been, but they were Presbyterians nonetheless. It was unlikely that their faces would be on any mural in the not-too-distant Loyalist streets for they are a part of our Protestant and Presbyterian heritage that some of us would like to deny or at best forget.

Henry Joy was a man of commitment whose yearning and desire for an Ireland that would be united was to take him to his death; a death, we are told, he faced with courage and determination. His sister, Mary Ann, distraught at the thought of losing her brother, not only gathered to watch but took her brother's arm to walk with him to the place of execution at the corner of Belfast's Cornmarket and High Street. Ordered to leave she refused to go, but Henry intervened. He kissed her and then seeing an old friend in the crowd, he said to him, 'Take poor Mary home'. At that moment the burden of her grief, clashing with her political commitment, was such that she needed a friend, someone to lean on, someone to walk with her. Henry Joy must have known the depth of what Mary Ann felt. He knew she needed a friend.

This is a story of love and commitment and courage, no matter whether we agree with the political sentiments which caused it to be written. It certainly adds new dimensions to the instruction of Paul to the Galatians that we should carry one another's burdens and in this way fulfil the law of Christ. Further depths are added to the instruction when we remember that there are bits of our history, from whichever aspiration we come, which we would like to disown for they are indeed a burden to us. Help to carry one another's burdens, and in this way you will obey the law of Christ.

Peace to be Made

Lesley Carroll

In 1775 Great Britain went to war with her American colonies. It wasn't long before France and Spain joined in to support the American cause. Stretched by the war, Britain made it clear that she could no longer be responsible for protecting Ireland and so it was that groups of volunteers were brought together to protect Ireland and defend her against any attack. Belfast took the lead in forming volunteer groups but it was no time until every village and town had their own company. People of every kind of social background joined the volunteers for there was no doubt that all shared a concern to defend their land. It is recorded that even Presbyterian ministers espoused the cause, and on Sunday mornings in Presbyterian pulpits it was possible to see men who made it clear that they were one of the volunteers.

'The rusty black was exchanged for the glowing scarlet, and the title "Reverend" for that of "Captain".'[1]

Ministers sometimes preached dressed in full uniform, laying aside their sword before preaching the sermon. The volunteers, gathered to worship, appreciated the often fiery and outspoken sermons which were delivered and often applauded the preacher.

War and peace, violence and non-violent action – these are themes which have occupied the Christian Church down through the centuries, and rightly so, for we follow one who came among us with the gospel of peace, to preach peace between God and people. It might truthfully be said that the Church has had an ambivalent attitude to war and indeed it might truthfully be said that this ambivalence is held with some difficulty, for the debate about war and peace continues throughout the denominations.

I was surprised to learn that the historic peace churches – Quakers, Mennonites and the like – don't provide army chaplains and this stands as a clear sign of their commitment to peace and to non-violent means. Their pacifist stance has been a challenge to other denominations and indeed to those who belong to no denomination.

No matter what our stance on war and peace, violence and non-violence; whether we argue for a pacifist position or take up a 'Just War' position, we share the same gospel and we read the same words of Jesus recorded in the gospel of Matthew: Blessed are the peacemakers, for they shall be called the children of God (Mt 5:9).

There is always peace to be made – peace between nations, peace between ethnic groups, peace among friends and families. Feuds to be settled and silences to be broken. There is no ambivalence here. The makers of peace, those who work and strive and long for peace, those who are faithful in the often long hard slog preparing the ground for the blossom of peace, can be sure that they will be known as the children of God.

1   Scripture Politics: Selections from the Writings of William Steel Dickson
     (Brendan Clifford, ed.), London, Athol Books, 1991, 16.

A Fresh Vision

Lesley Carroll

'Shall we live by memory or imagination?' It was a catchy quotation drawn from an anonymous source, serving the speaker's purpose and challenging those of us listening to jerk our minds into thinking new thoughts. It is the kind of quotation that exercises my mind for days, but as the days have passed I have become uncomfortable by the way in which this writer sets memory over against imagination. Are these two things not connected? Surely they were in the minds of the biblical prophets who invited their listeners to reach deep into the memory of their faith, not that they could live in the past but that the memories could inspire them for the next step as they set out on the next stage of their journey.

In Northern Ireland, we are moving forward on the journey of building peace among the people of this island and with the people of Great Britain. We are reviewing everything that can be reviewed, taking account of spending and budget, trying to imagine ways of putting our society together in order that we will live within reasonable, inclusive and realistic limits. Sometimes, though, the memories are just too strong, the memories of how we have hurt one another. In those times we need what imagination offers to us – a new view and a fresh vision precisely because the memories should tell us that we want something different.

In our ordinary lives too we come to significant times, events and experiences that mark another turning point on the journey of our lives. Sometimes these times coincide with world events – the election of a president, the downfall of a dictator, a horrific natural disaster. But mostly they are times in our lives that only a few close friends know about.

These are times when we are challenged with the task of reimagining our future because we are, quite simply, not satisfied with things as they are.

The church, the community of believers, is persistently invited by the gospel to imagine ways forward in a changing world. That imagining of ways forward occurs at every level, locally, nationally and globally, and is fired by a vision of God whose spirit is upon us, anointing us to bring good news to the oppressed; to bind up the broken-hearted; to proclaim liberty to the captives, and release to the prisoners; and to comfort all who mourn. It is God who inspires us with imagination, liberates us from deadening memory, blesses us with memory which inspires, and guides us by the Spirit to be people who bring good news, healing, freedom and comfort.

Robben Island

Geraldine Smyth

Anyone who has met Nelson Mandela speaks of his towering personality emanating forgiveness, joy, and a wide-embracing love. Many have marvelled at the scope and scale of his humanity. His capacity to work with former enemies called forth a new Rainbow Nation.

On a visit to South Africa recently, I went to Robben Island where Mandela had passed twenty-two of his twenty-eight years in prison. I had wanted to go there to remember and give thanks that the apartheid shackles were now smashed.

The isolation of the island; its harsh limestone landscape; the deliberate location of the actual prison on a part of the island cut off from view of the sea and the distant beauty of Table Mountain; the grim walls and cramped sunless cells – all this gave me a sharp insight into the phrase 'sensory deprivation'. The lime quarry where Mandela and his companions wielded their pickaxes, through sub-zero winter or remorseless summer heat, reduced us to silence. It was a purgatorial place.

Suddenly, half-hidden by a rock, a small buck stared down. Out of nowhere, sniffing, aloof – it stood like a living statement of freedom and a different world. A silent movement and the buck was gone. Imagination took over: images of purgatory not just as a 'place' of expiation, but of transformation and hope. I wondered if maybe on another such day, this buck or one of its hardy ancestors had appeared just so, kindling a spark in Mandela's mind, its free spirit communing with him that the mind is not manacled. Was that the day when a mucked-up cave in a quarry became a lecture theatre, when 'We became our own faculty with our own professors ... our own courses'?[1]

Although – in his typically understated words, 'teaching conditions were not ideal', was it out of the eager study and debate that Mandela's new vision was forged: 'my hunger for the freedom of my own people became a hunger for the freedom of all people, white and black.'[2]

Now Robben Island is open to visitors who come to bear witness to the past. Our guide was a young woman at pains to explain why her people had chosen neither the soft way of amnesty nor the remorseless cycle of revenge: 'Not to have chosen the way of truth and reconciliation would have delivered us over to the apartheid system for a second time, but this time, as perpetrators. We had no choice before. But today we have a choice.'

---

1 *Long Walk to Freedom: The Autobiography of Nelson Mandela*, op. cit., 454.
2 Ibid.

In Each Other's Hands

Geraldine Smyth

'It is a thought universally acknowledged, that a single man in possession of a good fortune must be in want of a wife.' So announced Jane Austen's opening line in *Pride and Prejudice* – the exam novel that we adored or despised, now reproduced several times over in film versions. The story turns on morals and manners. The temptation to pride or prejudice turns the heads, troubles the minds and upsets the lives of the central characters, and the story holds the mirror up to our own petty failings and aspirations. In unfaltering, polished prose, Austen unpicks the self-deceptions and lays bare the bargaining ploys at play in her characters' pursuit of love or social position. The irony is exquisite and rapier-sharp, giving the lie to any belief that nineteenth-century love and marriage was any more or less romantic or more or less fickle or faithful than in our twenty-first century. And yet, sociological data tells us that couples today are many times less likely than their forebears to remain with the person they married; that barely more than half of marriages stay the course.

Mr and Mrs Bennet, that all too solid couple, and their houseful of marriageable, or unmarriageable, daughters, and their acquaintances and would-be suitors signal to us that the human heart has always been fickle, social tastes contrary, and marriages not necessarily made in heaven. Attending weddings of friends and relations, we continue to marvel at the irrepressibility of human trust, against the evidence, expressed in a promise to be faithful till death. We are all aware of our own capacity to fail in our promises. Scepticism about anything permanent pervades our culture, not least about plighting one's troth. One dictionary definition of 'plight' denotes 'pledge', but beside that

– in brackets – is 'danger'. Pledging truth to one another is to risk our lives into one another's hands.

I think it was Rilke who said that we are the only beings that make promises. Not quite true. Paul insists – speaking of God's enduring relationship with the Jews as people of the First Covenant – that God never takes back his promises or revokes his choice (c.f. Rom 11:28-29). God is the first one to promise love forever. And because of this, the human heart never gives up on the possibility of an unconditional promise. That is why the writer of 1 John claims, 'Everyone who loves is born of God … those who live in love, live in God … if we love one another, God lives in us' (Jn 4:7).

Here is one of the most intense concentrations of love language ever penned. The one who comes to save us offers love unconditional, but also vulnerable even unto death. Love is God's initiative and name, and the divine promise is fulfilled, however we may fail. Within the divine promise there is always the grace of a new beginning, and in the end, happiness forever. It is a trust we can rely on.

Where Your Treasure Is

Geraldine Smyth

Taking a year out is a favoured practice now among young people, often when they finish school, before going on to college. But others who have been some years in the world of work are taking a leaf out of their book. This desire to seek fresh fields and pastures new may arise as a turning point when a crisis, such as losing one's job, becomes an opportunity to stand back, or let go of long-settled routines and structures of life. For some, a year out involves an inner journey or quest, or it may take the form of an actual pilgrimage.

At an ecumenical event in Coventry I met a couple: they were fifty-somethings and committed Methodists – I'll call them Jim and Joy. When my travel arrangements went askew, although they scarcely knew me, they unhesitatingly brought me home for the night and I had the chance to hear the whole story of the journey they had just made around Europe.

A few years previously, Jim lost his job when his factory was relocated to another country. The financial settlement included educational funding. So he abandoned his career as a draughtsman and embarked on a degree in horticulture. It was both an adventure and a dream fulfilled. For the third-year work experience, Jim, with Joy, devised a creative project – writing to owners of big houses with gardens and to war cemetery trusts offering to do labour in the gardens or cemeteries for several weeks, in exchange for board and lodging and the freedom to develop a written and photographic record of the learning experience. That evening – via their stories and the stunning portfolio record – I became part of their pilgrimage: the frugal living, the interaction with the earth, the travelling light. For as I witnessed something of the 'before, during and after' of their shared labour – overgrown gardens weeded, pruned and brought back to life and colour, fences mended, graves tidied and headstones restored, new friendships forged – I discerned something of the newness that had awakened in them. Their journey had provoked a re-evaluation of their previous suburban life and of their real needs and values. They had been surprised by the joy that sprang from setting aside possessions and preoccupations. The transformation of the gardens so evident in the portfolios was an emblem also of a transforming inner journey. The treasured goods and chattels they had so carefully stowed in the attic out of the way of incoming tenants, now three months after their return remained unpacked, as if impediments to the different current of freedom and abundant life they had savoured. As they waved me off at the airport the next day, I was full of gratitude for their hospitality, but even more for their unselfconscious reminder to me of the way of Jesus, that other pilgrim; that there are things more precious than possessions; that when we take nothing with us for the journey, unbidden gifts will come to us through strangers. 'Where your treasure is there your heart shall be' (Lk 12:34).

Mind What You Say

Lesley Carroll

The joyful freedom of after-school play is evident on the faces of the children playing in our streets when they get a sometimes rare blink of sunshine. Their minds are far from maths and English, French and German, never mind chemistry and the dreaded physics. I remember very little from those physics classes but one of the things I do remember is the wavy lines representing sound waves. They wriggled across my page to signify how sound gets from speaker to listener to make the necessary impact.

Now I'm told that sound communicated by wavy lines is what causes distortion and interruption and this is the day for digital sound. With the technology of digital communication, the fuzzy edges on our screens, the frustration of tuning in, the intrusive fizzing and popping will all be gone. Communication will be clear, sharp, sure and uninterrupted. It seems like we've got it all sewn up.

But we forget that between the words spoken and the words heard there lies a world of distortion which not even digital sound can cut out. In Lewis Carroll's *Through the Looking Glass*, Humpty Dumpty says to Alice, 'When I use a word, it means just what I choose it to mean – neither more nor less.'

His listener might equally have said, 'When I hear a word it means just what I choose it to mean – neither more nor less.'

I've often had that experience – going through a conversation, talking as if the other person understood, and then they say something which indicates, sometimes to my dismay, that they haven't got what I'm saying at all but have heard something entirely different.

None of us is responsible for how another person chooses to react. We have no control over the space between what is spoken and what is heard, but we do have control over what we say, over the words we use. And aware of that space which so often distorts, we have a responsibility to be as clear as we can so that our words cannot be taken and twisted or used to back up all sorts of crazy ideas.

Perhaps it was an awareness of the space between speaker and listener that urged Paul to write, 'So then, putting away all falsehood, let all of us speak the truth to our neighbours, for we are members of one another ... Watch the way you talk ... Say only what helps, each word a gift' (Eph 4:25-29).

Discovering Happiness

Lesley Carroll

Calendar Girls! A great night out. It was all there – the whole spectrum of human experience. From dying and death and the terrible grief and pain of parting to the deep love of marriage and the loyalty of friendship. These values underpinned the story of village women from Yorkshire who dared to let their imaginations stretch to make dreams come true and achieve even more than they had imagined.

Interesting sidelines of thought are there too. Helen Mirren's portrayal of the witty and enthusiastic, if not always taken seriously, Chris Harper, quite different from her role as Jane Tennison in *Prime Suspect*. Julie Walters' portrayal of Annie Clarke, whose husband's death brought the calendar into being, quite different from her portrayal of the mother in *Dinner Ladies*. But through it all the heart-warming story of human trust, sympathy, courage and love carries the audience from raptures of laughter to sorrow in death. The women of the small Yorkshire village stored up together an inheritance that would bring them happiness for many years to come.

Happiness is something we create for ourselves. That is one of the mottos of our age in which consumerism is everything – happiness can be bought, brought home from the shops, journeyed to by aircraft or built up out of nothing. And we believe we have the capacity to create it – if we work hard enough and earn enough money, or if we win the lottery, or if we make gain for ourselves in the claims culture in which we live. But again and again we run up against a wall, illusive happiness just across on the other side.

Calendar Girls reminds us of the truth we are often intent on avoiding – that our happiness is intricately bound up with others and mined in relationships with others. It is not known apart from human trust, sympathy, loyalty, compassion and courage. Happiness is not something we create for ourselves but something that is discovered in relationships with others.

That is likely what Jesus was trying to teach us in his Sermon on the Mount when he taught, blessed are the meek for they shall inherit the earth, or blessed are the poor in spirit, for theirs is the kingdom of heaven. There is a much greater inheritance to be had when we know the truth that happiness is not something we create by ourselves and for ourselves, but is something we discover together through experiences of trust, compassion, sympathy, loyalty and love.

What to Wear?

Lesley Carroll

Shop till you drop and you'll feel one hundred per cent better. A new wardrobe of clothes, something to wear for that special night out, or just something new to help you to feel better. It isn't always easy to find just the right thing, especially if you are small like me. Everything is too long, too big and cut to the wrong dimensions.

Getting rid of the old things isn't always easy either, for they become comfortable and give us a kind of homely feeling. So those new jeans are left hanging in the wardrobe and the old tattered and torn jeans put on again.

Paul invites the Colossian Church to get rid of the old ways and find new ones, like putting on new clothes that make a difference.

But now you must get rid of all these things: anger, passion and hateful feelings. No insults or obscene talk must ever come from your lips. Do not lie to one another, for you have taken off the old self with its habits and have put on the new self. This is the new being that God, its Creator, is constantly renewing in his own image, in order to bring you to a full knowledge of himself.

You are the people of God; he loved you and chose you for his own. So then, you must clothe yourselves with compassion, kindness, humility, gentleness and patience. Be tolerant with one another and forgive one another when any of you has a complaint against someone else. You must forgive one another just as the Lord has forgiven you. And to all these qualities add love, which binds all things together in perfect unity.

These new clothes fit everybody. They are cut to the shape and size that will fit us all and they are cut to bring a new edge to living. They are cut to create people who are admired for the depth of their character, not for superficial reasons. It is ours to give thanks to God for the way of life that fits us all. At times we might have to struggle with ourselves and persuade ourselves that these new clothes are, in fact, better than the old ones. But when we do put them on they make a difference, not only to us but to other people as well. No need for a completely new wardrobe season after season. No need to rush out to the shops for these new clothes. They are found with God who clothes us by the work of the Spirit with the garments of the new Kingdom.

Called by Name

Geraldine Smyth

In ancient times, a person's name denoted her innermost being and character. In some cultures a person goes by a public name, but another is given at birth or in a rite of passage, a name for close friends to tryst with, but kept secret from enemies and outsiders. The power deriving from such knowledge in the wrong hands could be dangerous, giving access to the inner soul of a person where they are most vulnerable. We read in the gospel that when Jesus is about to raise Lazarus from the dead, he called him in a loud voice by name. In our culture, naming is linked mainly with birth and new life. Parents search out a name to suit the little person or to call them after some worthy forebear. The name characterises and connects a person within community, and opens a gateway to life.

I recall two contrasting scenes in Steven Spielberg's film, *Schindler's List* – the first when the bewildered Jewish prisoners have just arrived at the concentration camp. They line up in front of endless rows of desks, at which officials cancel out their name and allocate a number. It is a de-humanising procedure – stripping each of the dignity conferred on them by their personal name. In a later scene, in an all-night race against time, the list of those who will be smuggled out is compiled. The de-humanising process is reversed, as name after name is spoken and written down. Name after name is sought for and spoken in the desperate anticipation of another Exodus. As name after name is uttered, life and salvation are wrenched from the very jaws of death.

I thought of those scenes when I visited the Holocaust Memorial to the Children in Yad Vashem. It was created around a ritual of naming the names of every child who had died, at what age, and in which concentration camp. The visual background was a darkened room. Lights reflecting against angled glass created the impression of millions of stars. The extermination of two million children could not erase the memory of God's promise to Abraham and Sarah that their descendants would outnumber the sands of the seashore or the stars in the sky (Gen 15:2-6; 17:15-16; 22:15-18. In the naming of their names the children are memorialised and continue to bear witness to God's covenant.

So too, in the refugee camps after the Battle of Kosovo, we witnessed moving scenes relayed by the media, of the naming of the dead and the naming of the living: joyfully announced names of survivors; names of the disappeared cried out in lament; names read out at speed by aid workers, of those who must without delay mount the waiting bus: the heartbreak or hope of exile.

We remember them all, the named and the nameless ones. We raise them up to the God who calls each one by their name, the God who says to them, 'I will not forget you; see I have written your name on the palms of my hands' (Is 49:15-16).

Central Station

Geraldine Smyth

Civilization began with cemeteries. I read that once in some book. Its meaning came home to me recently as I stood at a graveside in a Belfast cemetery. Gerald had been something of a recluse, and what is glibly called 'eccentric' – off-centre, different, odd. The reality behind the label was an independent man of interesting habits: a collector of old 78 records, a hoarder of vintage film reels and classic videos, who would talk for an hour non-stop about trains and railways whenever he found a ready ear – which wasn't often. Death had come suddenly, unprovided for.

Gerald's death and funeral might easily have passed with no relative knowing of it. As it happened, the day before, I had been in Belfast and bought a different daily paper, where I saw its short stark reference to Gerald's death, and an appeal for any relatives to come forward. Appalled, I recognised that the named person was my mother's cousin. In a matter of hours, other relatives were contacted, the family grave identified and opened, church and funeral arrangements completed.

At the funeral, next day, neighbours and relatives turned out. Two representatives of Northern Ireland Railways came to pay their respects to an erstwhile colleague. The disconnected strands of a life were coming together. Then the coincidences came home to me. Had I not bought the fateful newspaper at Central Station in Belfast en route to the train, and wasn't it just as the train chugged past Adelaide Station that I noticed the newspaper appeal – the same station where Gerald had once worked and about which he had loved to reminisce?

Coincidence or providence, God knows. God knows each one by name. And God's care was there in the recognition that even though he was gone from this life, family and friends and funeral mattered; God's care was there in the persistence of the policeman and the priest who took no end of trouble to trace some family; God's care was there in a particular relative – my sister, who, with no hesitation, took on the responsibility of the funeral for someone little known to her.

Civilization began with cemeteries, on the day when the ancestors first approached the dead with a kind of gentleness and solemnity; when the custom of the decent funeral was established, that human ritual of bridging earth to heaven; when kith and kin felt the need to come together – to name and remember, to honour and bless the connections with the one who had died.

Civilization began with cemeteries, with the impulse to gather round a graveside, to return the dead to a final resting place, to search for some pattern in the strands of a life, to exchange the word of regret or comfort, to pray together and to remember them before God.

Pilgrim Shoes

Geraldine Smyth

There are some among my friends who have a weakness for shoes. Strange things, shoes: hardly anything more down to earth and functional. Yet, designers seem to be endlessly creative in re-inventing old models – from courtiers' velvet pumps to buccaneer boots, to canvas deck shoes; imagining endless new possibilities from long-toed sling-backs to Doc Martens, and sneakers with lights that flash in the dark.

In literature of every time and culture we find the shoe symbol: the jack-boot standing for tyrannical regimes; or the worldly shoes Moses was instructed to remove on account of the ground he stood on being holy; it was because of a glass slipper, lost and found, that Cinderella walked free from her stepsisters' clutches into the open arms of her prince.

We recall Hans Christian Anderson's cautionary tale about the longing of a young girl for red shoes. Her longing turns to obsession. She covets and seeks chances to slip into the forbidden red shoes till she almost becomes them; dancing herself to the point of exhaustion, till her dancing feet lose the run of themselves, and in the end, she becomes a cripple. The tale signals the danger of running after conventional desires and fake 'stand-ins' for the deeper passion of one's true nature.

The battered old shoes in the Van Gogh painting suggest that he was someone who indeed walked where his true nature led. These were in fact the artist's own shoes, the ones in which he set out from home as a young man on a journey that was to transform his life. His destination was the seminary in a far distant town, where he intended to follow in his father's steps and study to be a pastor. But on the way, he came on a horrific mining accident. He broke off his journey so as to take care of an appallingly injured miner. Doctors claimed the miner was beyond hope. But Vincent nursed him night and day for many months with stubborn tenderness, until the man came back to life. The seminary course abandoned, Vincent instead had plumbed a well of unimaginable suffering and salvation. Nothing would be the same after.

Throughout his tortured life, Van Gogh kept the beaten-up shoes − a reminder of that journey, one that became a journey into God; a journey interrupted by saving grace, and the revelation that God's plan for him was not the mapped-out way of the pastor, but the risky holiness of the artist's pilgrimage. His true calling was to disclose the compassion of Christ through the fierce tenderness of his painting. In his own times of desperation, shabby boots were the clung-to sign that 'we are God's work of art, created in Christ Jesus for good works, which God prepared beforehand that we should walk in them' (Eph 2:10).

Advent & Christmas

Cleaning Up and Clearing Out

Lesley Carroll

You can always tell when I have become discontented and feel defocused from the necessary tasks of my life when I start cleaning up and clearing out. It has always reached rock bottom when I start to move furniture around. However little the distance the furniture is moved, it creates a space to stand in to view life in a slightly different way, to refocus and decide what the essential tasks really are. Everyone does this one way or another – programmes are taken off the air, reporters find themselves moved from one area of broadcast to another, teachers have in-service days, homemakers clean out the kitchen cupboards, chefs reshape the menus, some of us make lists, and some of us move furniture. We all have our own way of cleaning up and clearing out.

Churches too provide opportunities for cleaning up and clearing out. Members are provided with varieties of opportunities not just at Sunday worship but in other ways too. From the sale stalls decked out with things we have never used or clothes we have never worn, to the seasons of the Christian year, there is space created to clean up and clear out. Advent provides such a time: for waiting and preparing, for the self-examination that winter stillness encourages, until the point comes when the days are darkest, that we emerge to the joy of Christ with us and the celebration of our Saviour's birth.

Cleaning up and clearing out was perhaps on the mind of the person who wrote to the Hebrews long ago about laying aside every weight and chain and running with perseverance the race that is set before us. Whether we call it sin or a loss of focus or a mistake that repeats itself again and again in our lives, we all know the experience of gathering moss to slow us down, making the route bumpy and uncertain. Or it may feel like a build-up of lactic acid in the limbs, making them weigh a ton. But in the case of a life that hasn't begun to lay aside the weights and chains, then it isn't possible to simply run through the pain barrier.

Every now and again we need to pause in order to de-clutter. We need to give ourselves time to disentangle the chains that have wrapped themselves around our lives. We are killing ourselves if we don't. So before the tinsel takes over and the shops beckon once more, take some time during these Advent days to clean up and clear out so that you reach the high point, able to celebrate and to begin again, knowing that God is truly among us.

Ebenezer

Lesley Carroll

Christmas carols rang in Scrooge's ears, driving him deeper into grumpiness and loneliness as he allowed himself to be bound by the chains of his own making. How I love the story of old Ebenezer Scrooge and the changes that came to his life during the days before Christmas. His transformation is an ageless parable for this Advent time. It can awaken in us memories of lessons we have already learned, an awareness of challenges we have yet to face, a recognition of depths that we still need to plumb. Ebenezer's turnaround mirrors the longing for a better world that lives in all our hearts. It tells us that it is within our gift to make peace on this earth, to bring goodwill to people everywhere, to choose light and not darkness.

Within our hearts the ghost of Christmas past is stirred to life, bringing memories rich and plentiful of childhood Christmases. These memories awaken the longing for the traditional things of the season – the lights on the tree, the dancing flames of the fire, the candles on the mantelpiece and in the window. Out and about, the winter air tightens our breathing and each breath steams in front of us as we walk. The crisp night air and the piercing brightness of the stars lend themselves to our sense of anticipation. The frosty air hangs expectantly around the street lights and a smile rises on our lips as we await the celebration.

And there are so many preparations – the cake to bake, the pudding to make, a turkey to order, the presents to buy and to wrap. Children will have spent hours poring over the pages of magazines, talking to their friends, surfing the net – months avidly listening to advertisements in a bid to decide what tempting gifts are on offer this Christmas. The letters will have been sent to Santa and all that has to be done is to wait and see what will be left under the Christmas tree.

Soon the day will come and the reason for our excitement, our exchange of gifts, our lightness of step will be upon us – the day we celebrate the birth of Jesus Christ, the light of the world. Through him, we cannot tolerate the darkness. More than at any other time of the year, we are set upon the light and search out signs of the light: that which is seen in the bright eyes of excited children, the radiant lights of the city and the light of love and hope born in our hearts. All blend to remind us of the true light who would dispel darkness from the world.

So, during this time of anticipation, let's try to make that journey from darkness to light in our hearts, in our words and in our deeds. Let's make the same journey as Ebenezer Scrooge – the cranky old man who was changed by the new light that came to him at Christmas-time.

Their Fears, Our Fears

Lesley Carroll

As we each make our personal Advent journey to Bethlehem, we carry with us all our burdens, fears and anxieties. Mary and Joseph, who made that journey ahead of us, brought their own burdens to the birthplace of Jesus. It is easy to overlook the emotional storm they encountered as we view the serene figures in the Christmas crib. How different their reality must have been.

Mary's Thoughts:
It's been such a long journey. Thank God the end is in sight. I am so weary of travel; weary of carrying this child, bones aching, head throbbing, wondering if we will ever make it to Bethlehem. The time is near. I've been so willing, but as the time gets near I feel overwhelmed; after all, he is my son too and I have to give him the best love I can and the best guidance for his life. This child will change my life. I have seen my friends have children and their lives changed completely, overnight.

But my life is already so changed — changed by this news. I am not who I was. I am not so certain of myself, so settled in my future, content in anonymity. I am changed and my relationships have changed. My son is to be great and he will do wonderful things. People will know me as his mother. They may all call me 'blessed' but will I ever feel understood or listened to again? I am so afraid of the loneliness that is to come.

How far away and strange and unreal it all seemed when I went to visit Elizabeth and shared the news with her. I could hardly believe what I was hearing from the angel. I had to test it out on someone and I had to know the truth of the pregnancy for myself. Then to discover that Elizabeth was pregnant too and that she had feelings like I had, feelings of uncertainty and surprise and wonder and fearfulness. It was good, to have someone understand the strangeness of it all. And when the child she was carrying moved with such vigour when I arrived, then I had no doubt it was true — this child I carry, this child sheltered by my tired body and fed by my dwindling resources, is to be the Son of God.

The Son of the Most High God, and I his mother. I am to hold him in my arms. I am to wash and feed him. I am to watch his first few steps and worry about him when he is out playing with his friends. I am to teach him how to be a son in the tradition of our family and religion. I share with Joseph this heavy responsibility. I hope I won't let him down.

Joseph's Thoughts:
Dear God, she looks so weary. So much has threatened to come between us since this news — people disbelieving and mocking, family not understanding, neighbours talking, to say nothing of my own doubts. I am ashamed of my doubts, ashamed that I could even think, however fleetingly, of doubting her word, of leaving her alone. I love her and I know her. No matter how often I say 'forgive me', the doubts linger. I look in her face and see the one I love, but also one who is a stranger to me. So strong, so certain, so accepting. I never knew she had such inner strength.

I wonder if anyone understands what this has done to me and could yet do to me. But I can't let the disappointment and doubt get in the way. If this child truly is the Son of the Most High God, if he really is the one whom we have been waiting for, then I want joy and delight, not bitterness and anger. I want to dance and sing, not weep and mourn. I don't want to be excluded from this time, from this birth.

If only we didn't have to make this journey to Bethlehem, but we have no alternative. I have to go back to my own town to register and I can't leave her at home. We could do without it and I worry about Mary and the child. The child ... when I see the face of that little one, then will I know? Will I see such love dancing from his eyes and flowing from his smile that I will have no doubt left? Will this indeed be the moment for which we have been waiting? Will this be the hour of grace?

We have far to go yet. We have time to wait. I hope this will be a journey of grace, lightened by hope and not just haunted by fear — a journey of grace for Mary and for me.

Stories

Geraldine Smyth

Tomás Ó Criothfain was the great storyteller of the Blasket Islands. But, as he grew old, no story could be coaxed from him, even by his old friend from England, Robin Flower. Finally, Ó Criothfain explained to him that the newspapers were now coming across from the mainland with all their 'little stories', and that these little stories had driven the 'Big Story' out of his head.[1]

John the Baptist is the larger-than-life figure at the edge of Christmas, proclaiming, 'Repent, the reign of God is at hand'. Mary, that robust woman, takes on the proportions of a prophet, heading into the hill country to visit Elizabeth. Hill country, not rolling pasture, recalls the rugged command, 'Get thee up into the high mountain!' These words of God to Isaiah (Is 40:9), after countless more performances of 'The Messiah', have had the roughness rolled out of them, perhaps. The prophet Ezekial upbraids those false prophets who have 'not gone up into the gaps' (Ezek 13:5). Writer, Annie Dillard, assents: 'The gaps are the thing. The gaps are the Spirit's one home ... The gaps are the clifts in the rock where you cower to see the back parts of God ... ' Go into the gaps, she tells us, 'if you can find them.'[2]

In some traditions, an empty chair is placed at the Christmas table, memory to absent friends. Or a space is left for the proverbial stranger to be welcomed as special guest. Christmas is the feast of the outsider called in from the cold, a time for the homeless to find a home. Christmas calls us to face into the gaps in our hearths and in our hearts, in our churches and communion tables.

There are so many little stories that drive the big story out of our heads: stories of shopping till we're dropping; bus queues and the rush to parties; songs in supermarkets of winter wonderlands and of Mammy kissing Santa Claus underneath the mistletoe. A far cry from the rough hospitality of Bethlehem, birthplace of the Big Story: at the year's deep midnight, unexpected dawn; the people that walked in darkness have seen a great light; Word made flesh. This big story draws us to look out for the left-out and to listen for mystery in unsuspected places.

We need some little silence to receive God's gift of Jesus, the revelation of God's all-embracing love. In the blazing light of that big story all the little stories can shine out transformed – stories of last-minute cards, visits to folk cut off by sickness or poverty from the seasonal merriment; frantic secrecies of large presents stowed in small roof spaces; the rush to school concerts or carols at the local residence for the elderly. Amid all the commerce and crowds by such gestures we share ourselves with those who see little of life's blessings – as we are all drawn into the feast of heaven's marriage to earth, revealed in a mother's love and a child's face:

This baby lies
Wrapped in rags
Is fed by a girl
O if God begs
Then we all hold

Him in our power
We catch our breath.[3]

1   See Robin Flower, *The Western Island; or the Great Blasket*, with illustrations by Ida M. Flower, Oxford, Clarendon Press, 1944.

2   Annie Dillard, *Pilgrim at Tinker Creek*, New York, HarperPerennial Books, 1985 (1975), 269.

3   Elizabeth Jennings, 'Christmas Suite in Five Movements': no. 2 'The Child', in *Moments of Grace*, Manchester, Carcanet Press, 1979, 59.

This Birth

Geraldine Smyth

Six hundred years ago, the great teacher, Meister Eckhart, quoting St Augustine in one of his renowned 'German Sermons', asked, 'What does it avail me if this birth is always happening, if it does not happen in me? That it should happen in me is what matters.'[1] Eckhart was reminding us that we are all characters in the story of the birth of Christ; we are not spectators but participants.

The birth of Jesus stretches our sense of who we are and what we stand for. God pitches tent among us, and calls us to widen the site of our tent (Is 54:2). If the birth of Jesus does not upset our narrow views, our prejudiced ways of talking or refusing to talk, it is no more than a sentimental story under fairy lights on synthetic Christmas trees.

Birth, as we know, is a disturber of old routines. But St Matthew's story of the birth of Jesus is shot through with the terror of Herod's slaughter of the Israelite children. Lament rends the air. The sky is red-tinged at Jesus' birth, the earth 'christened' with tears:

> A voice was heard in Ramah,
> wailing and loud lamentation,
> Rachel, weeping for her children,
> she refused to be consoled,
> because they are no more. (Mt 2:18)

In our land in our own day, Rachel still weeps. Peace emerges in suffering for what is lost, lament for those who are no more. Like the magi in T.S. Eliot's poem,[2] we have journeyed far and hard, and we can say with them, '... this Birth was/Hard and bitter agony for us, like Death, our death.' The birth of peace leaves us changed and at times confused: we are '... no longer at ease here, in the old dispensation'.[3] But the risk of searching out a different route can be a scary prospect. We all stand in need of healing and fresh courage to make the unprecedented moves, now, not later. If not now, when?

This birth of peace, for all its pain, brings hope and heralds joy. This birth brings healing in its wings. No-one need be outsider to this joy – shepherds, kings, believers, unbelievers, foreigners, friends, them and us, you and me. Swords will be hammered into sickles. Weapons laid aside will make space for welcomes. Such peace is not handed down to us by our ancestors or by the powerful of this world. This peace is offered by a small child. It is on loan to us from our children and from our children's children.

1   Meister Eckhart: Sermons and Treatises, Vol. 1, Sermon 1, op. cit., 1–13, 1.

2   'The Journey of the Magi', T.S. Eliot: The Collected Poems and Plays, op. cit., 103–104, 104.

3   Ibid.

New Town, Ancient City

Geraldine Smyth

I wonder sometimes who it was that invented the notion of new towns – the idea of beginning all over again fresh; new people, new houses, desk-top housing estates. Wipe the slate clean and away we go to fabricate a future. But we have heard too of the alienation felt by families who have had to uproot and transplant themselves far from kith and kin; away from the old street and country customs of familiar places with all their ill-sorted quirkiness and characters.

A while ago on the radio, I heard of one such experiment: a fifty-thousand-acre site close to Disneyland, California, was to become a new town named Celebration. The allotments were being snapped up, they said, for this was to be a new town with a difference, because folk going to live there were to enjoy the comforts and hygiene of life with all mod-cons. But part of the sunny package was that they would also buy into a Victorian value system of decency, sobriety and upright living. Security guards on every street corner would see to it that crime was non-existent. Here was a vision of law and order and moral cleanliness, an exclusive club – the very opposite of the gospel, quite at odds with the Incarnation. American writer, Annie Dillard, is someone for sure who will not be buying property in Celebration. In her book, *Pilgrim at Tinker Creek*, she exults in nature's intricacy, rejoices that its unruliness refuses to be tamed. 'That something is everywhere and always amiss is part of the very stuff of creation'.[1] In fact, 'It's chancy out there'.[2]

Coming up to Christmas, many minds turn to an ancient city crammed with people from all arts and parts; raggeds and royals, summoned by a census, taking their chances in hostelries and boarding houses, messing up the place every which way. Among them, temporarily housed in a cave, were Joseph and Mary, vagrants from Nazareth. There in Bethlehem, Jesus, the Son of God, came into a world rough-edged and fearsome, and made it his own.

Bethlehem, where even new-born infants had to fear for their lives. Bethlehem, City of David, that passionate man, who in sin and repentance for his sin learned the measure of himself and learned the measurelessness of God's forgiving love. Bethlehem, city where God found a way into the labyrinth of human lawlessness and a way through it. Bethlehem, city where Jesus is vulnerable as a small baby and reveals to us that forever after, God's divine face will shine out in the bits and bobs of every day; for God's new creation is here, now within us, among the well and the wounded, inviting the law-keepers and the law-breakers. God's word brings comfort to all the Rachels of the world whose tears cry out in Ramah or Darkley, or Loughinisland or Shankill or Enniskillen or Dublin, because her children are no more. Bethlehem is Belfast or Bosnia, Birmingham or Azerbaijan, Darfur or Baghdad ... and the bright star of Bethlehem shines over us all.

1   Dillard, *Pilgrim at Tinker Creek*, op. cit., 180.
2   Ibid., 171.